"Don and Fran have mastered the art of leading with purpose, values, and story . . . and now they're giving you the playbook."

—*Larry Weber, chairman and CEO of Racepoint Global and Founder of Weber Shandwick*

"This important book is a must-read for every leader striving to build a successful values-based organization."

—*Doug Fletcher, co-Author of How Clients Buy*

"Defining your purpose is no longer optional. That's table stakes. It's not easy, but it's simple. Where the real magic (and the real work) lies is ensuring your people not only understand your purpose but also how to live and breathe it every day. That's the hard part, but this book gives you the roadmap."

—*Deborah Leff, IBM CTO | Data and AI*

"Travel is complex; every day, Delta transports millions of travelers across the globe. The only way to make that happen is to align people around our purpose, values, and story. This book will guide you to uncover your Three Keys".

—*Henry Kuykendall, Delta, senior vice president*

"For over two decades, Gallup has studied how individual strengths impact organizations. In this book, Don and Fran explain the three critical organizational strengths that impact your company and the world. The Three Keys form a strong foundation for any organization to thrive."

—*Maika Leibbrandt, Gallup, senior executive*

"20 years ago, David Maister taught us how to manage a professional services firm. Now, it's all about leadership. Leading with your purpose, values, and story will change everything. This book will show you how."

—*Cliff Farrah, CEO and president, The Beacon Group*

"This book is an insightful work of art. Rather than write empty words like so many others, Don and Fran opt to deliver deep substance, with practical application. I recommend this vital resource to the leaders of any organization, as leaders of all industries require clear and concise methodology like Don and Fran's to captivate the hearts of employees and customers alike."

—*Kipp Marcus, director of Core Marketing, Amazon Europe*

"Don and Fran's vast knowledge of the next generation of buyers, share-holders, and employees is the most useful to date. If I had read a book like this years ago, I'd have led the companies I founded to even greater success at an even quicker pace."

—*Jeff Herzog, founder and former CEO of iCrossing and ZogDigital*

"When executives used to transition to new jobs, roles, and companies, they always evaluated the location, compensation, and opportunity. Now more than ever, they consider things like purpose and values. If you want to attract and retain the best executives, you need to know and live your vision. To do that, you need this book."

—*George Bradt, Prime Genesis chairman/founder, author of First Time Leader, The New Leader's 100-Day Action Plan, and CEO BootCamp*

"If you want to break sales records and build national firms for success, read this book. This guide for growth is as effective as any work I've ever written, if not even more so. The opportunity to learn and leverage Don and Fran's genius masterwork is one that no business leader can afford to pass up."

—*Jack Daly, serial entrepreneur, bestselling author, and internationally recognized business coach*

"My book with Tom McMakin explained *how* clients buy. In this book, Fran and Don beautifully articulate *why* clients buy. This important work is a must-read for every leader striving to build a successful values-based organization."

—*Doug Fletcher, co-author of How Clients Buy*

"While I've studied the lasting impact of social media on today's customers, Don and Fran have analyzed how the global movement toward corporate purpose has forever changed the way customers think. Together, the expert authors created their own masterplan for leading businesses and institutionalizing success in this ever-evolving world. Their ambitious collection of pivotal insights represents the latest thinking in marketing and overall leadership of organizations across industries. Today's leaders must explore intellectually stimulating and outright inspiring texts like this one to build their brand loyalty and gain the irresistibility that every business seeks."

—*Dave Kerpen, chairman of Likable Media and award-winning author*

"I've been an employee of Investis US since the beginning. I witnessed the ups and downs that we experienced in early efforts to adapt to the market. However, under Don's purposeful leadership, we've seen nothing but immense growth. With the principles clearly defined in Don and Fran's book, success in changing times is now within every leader's grasp."

—*Melissa Davis, senior director U.S. Operations, Investis Digital*

"Working with Don Scales is always a profitable journey that will move your company rapidly from one successful venture to the next opportunity. Don's effective technique, paired with Fran's proven approach, can launch any career and build any business in a time when others struggle to. I hope everyone will read this to get a real taste of the meaningful and lucrative world you can live in if you lead with the Three Keys."

—*David Corchado, chief digital officer of Investis Digital*

"I can say from firsthand experience that Fran's methods are highly effective in expanding a business's reach. I've led not one, but two organizations that have grown exponentially, since Fran helped us brand and rebrand with the Three Keys. They flat-out work. Paired with Don's clear professional services mastery, their playbook is the perfect tool to help you repeat your success."

—*Jumana Salem, head of projects for Aleph Education*

"I would personally recruit any leader with half the brilliance this book has to offer. The book not only provides a unique perspective on leading professional services firms but also masterfully compiles a myriad of crucial information that leaders can simply apply to lead any business organization in a shifting market."

—*Jay Hussey, CEO, SRI North America*

"Great leaders are great storytellers. They know when, how, and why to tell their stories in order to attract top talent, build meaningful relationships, and swiftly grow organizations. If you aspire to accomplish any of that, give this book a read. Their story will shape yours."

—*Robert Wagnon, CEO of Republic State Mortgage*

"Over my ample experience in leadership positions at top companies, I've never come across another leader like Don Scales. I personally watched as Don proved purpose is absolutely necessary to produce profit in the current market. On more than one occasion, he has initiated purposeful changes to broaden our team of experts and uplift our services. Your business, too, will thrive if you can successfully infuse meaning and values into everything you do, and this book discloses how."

—*David Grigson, chairman of Investis Digital*

"Fran laid out the groundwork for my consulting firm's brand and has helped us thrive with purpose in the years since. The sensible ideas she and Don brilliantly described in this book have never ceased to provide serious improvements to our business and I hope everyone reads this book to reap the benefits that we have."

—*Greg Crabtree, CEO and* Simple Numbers *author*

"This essential leadership manual accurately captures the most crucial elements of creating a high-performance organization. Your purpose, values, and story are fundamental to gaining a competitive advantage in today's market place. Any leader who aims to unify and advance their organization today stands to benefit from internalizing Don and Fran's ideas."

—*Warren Rustand, CEO of Summit Capital Consulting*

"There is no one better than Don Scales to write a book on leading successful professional services firms. I've seen with my own eyes his ability to transform companies into highly profitable, global businesses that people are proud to work for and with. Blending his experience with Fran's Three Keys framework, this book provides the ultimate blueprint for corporate leadership."

—*Kristen Kalupski, VP of Marketing at Investis Digital*

"Having experienced both Fran's workshop and marketing expertise, I'm eternally grateful for the invaluable insights she has given me. The resources that Fran offers undoubtedly enabled me to connect with and help many of the clients that I have. Now, the purposeful business bible that she and Don put together sums up the critical information for you to start to design your business, gain traction, and achieve your vision."

—*Cesar Quinterio, visionary CEO of Fit2Go*

"I can personally attest to the tremendous shareholder value generated by the Three Keys framework. This book's vital insights make it the ultimate source to study for anyone serious about leadership and growth."

—*Andrew Paul, Enhanced Equity Fund (former investor in iCrossing)*

"Nonprofit organizations like my own must inspire people in order to reach them. While our mission has always been crucial, Fran's rewarding techniques have enabled us to reach new heights and touch more lives than ever before. She helped us uncover and share our foundation to double the size of our client and donor base. Now, with this book, she and Don will do the same for you."

—*Zvi Gluck, director of Community Resources, Amudim*

"As a longstanding board member for a company led by Don Scales, I could not help but be impressed by the excellent results he consistently creates. I am certain that our surplus in revenue can be largely credited to the purpose-driven leadership methods that Don and Fran accurately describe with actionable terms in their book. Given my experience, I'd quickly recommend a read to anyone who wants to better understand how to lead a professional services organization, or any business at all in our purpose-driven world."

—*Richard Chapman, partner/lead investor in Investis Digital*

"Fran has an unparalleled understanding of what you need to achieve enduring success in any business. Her Three Keys workshop shined a light on a new way of thinking for me. It reinvigorated my passionate love for the work I do and thereby revitalized my performance. I left inspired to share that impact with others, and the lessons I took from it have stayed with me to this day. I'd encourage everyone who can to read this book. It genuinely will drive your purpose and profit."

—*Luly B. Carreras, founder of Luly B. Consultancy*

"Having closed roughly 40 merger-and-acquisition deals, I recognize genuine expertise when I see it. Without a doubt this book is one of the best I've read at articulating how to envision a thriving organization and deliver upon that vision in these purpose-driven times. Don and Fran lay out a leadership style that will give anyone in any company a sense of confidence about the future, during transitions and always. This book is the best education available today for anyone looking to acquire or lead any organization."

—*Mike Jackson, former CFO at Agency.com and iCrossing*

How to Lead
a Values-Based
Professional
Services Firm

How to Lead a Values-Based Professional Services Firm

3 Keys to Unlock Purpose and Profit

DON SCALES & FRAN BIDERMAN GROSS

WILEY

Library of Congress Cataloging-in-Publication Data:

Names: Scales, Don, author. | Biderman-Gross, Fran, author.
Title: How to lead a values-based professional services firm : 3 keys to unlock purpose and profit / Don Scales, Fran Biderman-Gross.
Description: Hoboken, New Jersey : John Wiley & Sons, Inc., [2020] | Includes bibliographical references and index.
Identifiers: LCCN 2019041160 (print) | LCCN 2019041161 (ebook) | ISBN 9781119621522 (hardback) | ISBN 9781119621539 (adobe pdf) | ISBN 9781119621553 (epub)
Subjects: LCSH: Professional corporations—Management.
Classification: LCC HD62.65 .S33 2020 (print) | LCC HD62.65 (ebook) | DDC 658.4/092—dc23
LC record available at https://lccn.loc.gov/2019041160
LC ebook record available at https://lccn.loc.gov/2019041161

Cover Design: Wiley
Cover Image: © Fran Biderman-Gross and Don Scales

Printed in the UK by TJ International Ltd, Padstow, Cornwall

10 9 8 7 6 5 4 3 2 1

Dedication

It all began with a single vision in our tiny garage on 69th Road. David Biderman never did anything small. Even though he has been gone now for more than 18 years, I feel he has been guiding me all along this journey. He wouldn't be surprised at all about our accomplishments. Actually, I truly believe he would have expected it. The untimely passing of my dad, the inestimable Bernie Leff, just weeks before publishing this book, leaves me without my biggest fan. While he was always filled with unparalleled pride, like David, none of my vast accomplishments ever surprised him—until I completed this book. I take solace in knowing that even now, he cheers me on, from above.

—Fran

Anything I accomplish in life must be attributed to the inspiration provided by my parents. My mother was always there with the perfect words of encouragement and a belief in her only child that was second to none. Her words, "Someone is going to come in first today, I see no reason it can't be you," are motivational words that I still carry with me every day. And my dad was such an amazing parent, friend, and human being that to do anything other than your best for him would be a personal disappointment. But today, both are smiling and saying, "That's our boy."

—Don

Contents

Contents

About the Authors

Fran Biderman Gross gets people noticed so that their true potential can be revealed. As the CEO and founder of Advantages—an award-winning, New York–based end-to-end communications agency—she leads her clients on an invaluable journey of brand discovery that reveals their personal and organizational Three Keys: purpose, values, and story.

Fran's firm Advantages is a paradigm for the Three Keys as their shared values are infused into every action. Every client interaction and every project is an opportunity to demonstrate how to bring purpose forward into marketing, branding, leadership, and culture. Since 1992, Advantages has blossomed from a local printing business to multi-million dollar powerhouse branding and marketing agency that serves clients across the globe. Advantages is an *Inc.* 500 fastest-growing company and has been named one of *Inc.*'s 50 Best Places to Work. Advantages' client work consistently garners industry awards and recognition.

Fran excels at leading senior executives to clearly see the results from purpose-driven approaches to marketing and leadership. She synthesizes decades of marketing expertise into inspiring and actionable steps so that purpose-oriented leaders can empower their teams and their organizations to build enduring emotional connections with their markets.

Her proprietary Three Keys and Spark Purpose workshops have inspired thousands of executives to achieve greater clarity, alignment, and impact by using the Three Keys to unlock their stories. The results of working with Advantages are revealed in increased market share, improved client and employee retention, and overall revenue growth.

Fran is an Executive Board Member of the Queens Chamber of Commerce, Women in Print, and the Charna Radbell Foundation, as well as an active member of the Entrepreneurs' Organization. She frequently lectures at universities and is a sought-after speaker at entrepreneurial, women-, and industry-focused conferences and events. She graduated from MIT's Entrepreneurial Master's Program and Goldman Sachs' 10,000 Small Businesses program. She lives in New York with her Tony award–winning husband, Yeeshai Gross, and their family.

For more than three decades, **Don Scales** has run professional services firms and understands firsthand how to make them succeed. In his current role as global CEO of Investis Digital, he is executing on his vision to lead a company unlike anything else in the digital communications space. He's put together a team with deep expertise in corporate communications and investor relations, and united them with innovative performance marketing experts and world-class technology solutions to help companies connect with audiences across all digital touchpoints.

Since Don joined in 2016, the company has seen exponential growth. In 2018, he spearheaded a rebranding of the business, including a new name, Investis Digital, that reflects the focus on delivering sustained value by helping clients connect with their customers through digital. In 2019, he led the launch of Connect.ID, an innovative technology platform that makes it possible for businesses to develop content that connects with their audiences across a rapidly expanding digital universe in a secure fashion. Now the company has 9 global offices and 2,000 clients, including Ascential, ASOS, Fruit of the Loom, Rolls-Royce, and Wyndham.

Don previously led iCrossing from a small search agency to a global full-service digital agency that was acquired by Hearst Corporation for over $300 million. Prior to that, he was CEO of Omnicom Group's Agency .com, where he successfully led the company through a tremendous period of growth. He has also served as Managing Director of Igate Capital, as well as Group Vice President of Industry Consulting of Oracle and Senior Vice President of Management Consulting of EDS.

In addition to his MBA from Harvard Business School, he has dual undergraduate degrees in Chemical Engineering and Mathematical Physics, and a Master of Chemical Engineering from Rice University.

How to Lead a Values-Based Professional Services Firm

Introduction

Twenty or thirty years ago, businesses did not think about why they sold the services or products they did. Business owners and C-level executives did not give much thought, if any, to their firms' beliefs and values. Conventional wisdom at the time was simply "we provide a service to our clients in a professional manner, and they pay us accordingly." Profits were determined by how effectively and efficiently executives ran the firm. Until now, there was none better at explaining all this to us than David Maister in his seminal work, *Managing the Professional Service Firm*.

From a management standpoint, those practices are still valid, and no one was more respected than Maister, but there is a missing strategic piece: *brand foundation*. While running a business in the 21st century, particularly with regard to brand and culture, we find a drastically different world since Maister's work—for companies, employees, and customers. People want to know what you stand for and what you believe in, because it is no longer enough to work with a firm that offers excellent services; clients want to work with firms which align with their own beliefs and values. Customers want more than a transaction; they seek conversation and collaboration. Like any leader of a professional services firm, you probably focus on growth goals, increased sales, and streamlined efficiencies to increase profitability. We offer a different perspective: if you shift your focus to running a purpose-led, values-based company, all those things fall into strategic alignment at an expedited pace.

To be clear, in order to thrive in the 21st century, you must run all aspects of your business through the lens of your brand foundation. We will teach you how to lead from this lens, but first, we are going to talk about something nobody tends to talk about when first growing their company: how imperative it is to understand what your company believes in and why it was created. Do this and you have a chance. Do not do this and you will be building the company in proverbial quicksand, and it will become increasingly harder to lead your employees and clients as the business scales.

Maybe you would like to know who we are and why you should listen to us? Let's get that established first!

Half a Century of Combined Experience

We have decades of experience between us across numerous industries. I (Don) have led professional service firms for thirty-five years, in all shapes and sizes, and you will hear about my various experiences throughout the book. I did not always use the terminology "Three Keys," but knowing what my company does and why it exists has been the differentiator to my consistent success. After years of reflecting on how I got to where I was, in 2018, I discovered a hidden framework I had been executing all along without even realizing it. And, that is where Fran comes in—she has developed a reliable, repeatable framework for understanding what your company does and why establishing your Three Keys anchors all long-term, scalable success. She helped me see clearly what I had been doing, and I—no, we—want you to see the path forward clearly, too. Don't get me wrong. Ultimately, I would have been successful with my approach all alone. But Fran's approach supercharged the direction I was headed via Three Keys: purpose, values, and story. The keys gave me a new, different perspective on how to look at myself, my organization, and my employees. Before Fran, I knew how this stuff worked—by instinct and intuition—but post-Fran I now know how to communicate a repeatable framework for success that any executive leading a professional services firm will benefit from implementing.

I (Fran) started exploring the question of *why* we do what we do in 2001. I did not have a framework—yet—but instinctively, I understood it wasn't enough for companies just to produce a pretty brochure or logo; the way they communicated to their customers had to have meaning and purpose. After several iterations over four years, I developed a full-circle, 360-degree methodology that starts with purpose and strategically infuses that purpose into the values and story of the organization—hence the Three Keys.

I've been successfully implementing the Three Keys framework inside clients' businesses since 2005. Don was able to reap the benefits across his organization, further and faster than most clients because he had already instinctively internalized the framework before we ever met. When he saw the framework laid out as a strategic process, he understood its value immediately. Don had been executing the framework implicitly all along. I was not just working on the framework for the sake of selling a value-added service; I had been using and iterating the framework inside my own professional services firm, too. Whether you're running a large corporation or an entrepreneurial startup, embrace the Three Keys to anchor your brand foundation—and you will lead your company to faster, long-lasting, and more profitable success.

We're Not in the Business We Think We Are

A bit of background: Currently, I (Don) am CEO of a global digital communication company named Investis Digital. Before I arrived, Investis (as it was named then) was a digital communications company supporting the Investor Relations (IR) and corporate communications communities out of the United Kingdom. In 2014, the company decided to enter the U.S. market, where they were virtually unknown. Historically, the company had worked with publicly held companies in the U.K. to provide shareholder information on the companies' public websites, and the United States was a relatively new market for them. After two years, they had not gained the significant traction in the United States they had expected, and the board members were growing short on patience.

In 2016, I was brought in as the North American CEO to get their U.S. endeavor on track and to do so profitably. My job had the potential to be either very long-term or extremely short. We struggled in the United States throughout much of 2016, really not understanding what business we were in and how to make money doing it. We made some progress, but not the amount the board and I had expected to. In December 2016, my life at Investis took yet another turn. The board asked me to step into the role of global CEO. Virtually overnight my commute increased from a five-minute, three-block walk to a seven-hour transatlantic flight to London and back twice per month!

After immersing myself inside the global operations at Investis for several months, I was concerned about the direction of the company and how we were to differentiate, especially in the United States So, I organized a strategy meeting with my extended management team and the board in London to discuss these concerns. As you can imagine, the days leading up to this all-hands-on-deck meeting were extremely stressful. Many senior employees in London had been there for quite some time and had conventional fixed views on what Investis was as a company. My point to everyone was simple: "We need to look at the company in a different way. We are not in the IR business, like most of you think we are. We are not in the corporate communications business, like many of you think we are. If you take a step back and search with a different lens, we are in the content—the storytelling—business." It was true! We helped global clients build meaningful and enduring relationships with their stakeholders through engaging content.

To succeed, we had to adapt to how the world of communications had changed. We needed to think about ourselves as content specialists. We needed to bolster our content development capabilities and rethink how we optimized content for targeted impact, from how prospective clients found us all the way to how we distributed the content for consumption.

In a somewhat unexpected move to many at the time, I suggested we buy a performance marketing company. In my mind, I knew this strategy would not initially be an easy sell to an already frustrated board of directors. Nonetheless, after I had refocused their hearts and minds on a clear direction, they approached the potential acquisition with an open mind. Once they saw my vision for the synergistic value of performance marketing in conjunction with our existing digital communications capabilities, I received board approval to move forward. Investis acquired ZOG Digital at the end of 2017, and soon after we renamed our combined companies Investis Digital. No one else in the global market has such a unique set of core strategic capabilities. We literally redefined how businesses connected with their audiences online. It was at that precise point that we began to discuss rebranding the company to reflect our new identity and positioning as a single integrated global company.

Rebranding gave us an opportunity to create waves of momentum and energy around the new company's strategic vision, mission, and direction. It was the perfect excuse to reengage with every employee from all of our offices. As a first step, we launched a thirty-day logo competition to see which group could come up with the most compelling design. Each of our three offices—London, New York, and Phoenix—would propose a new logo, and we would get one external proposal as well.

Not Just a Logo

In looking for an external proposal from a branding professional, our head of marketing found Fran and her company, Advantages, through his network. Fran and her team brought a holistic and purposeful methodology to our new brand called Investis Digital. Just like the office teams, Fran and her team were tasked to design a logo, but Fran had a different approach: she wanted to spend time getting to know us before she put pen to paper. She picked my brain over the course of several calls, asked unconventional questions, looked at all of our previous brand- and culture-related documents, and sparked conversations with people throughout the company. Fran asked the type of questions I asked myself when thinking about the type of company we were and how we wanted to grow market share. She was curious about what we believed in, what we deemed valuable, and very politely challenged what we stood for.

When Fran and her team presented the logo (Figure I.1), I knew it was the winner as soon as I saw it. The logo had personality; it was immersively engaging and uniquely creative. The work that she and her team did provided new layers of meaning and context about the company. In addition to the logo, Fran drafted a compelling story about what Investis Digital stood for—and the story was spot on. It was unanimously clear to the committee that Fran's logo was the best choice.

I was intrigued: How had she—an outsider—captured our essence so quickly and so accurately? I knew my company because I was on the inside day in and day out. But in just a few short weeks, somehow Fran had codified and elegantly distilled our essence. I wanted to learn how she was able to capture and articulate something seemingly so hard for the rest of my team to grasp. I understood it, but leadership is not about what I understand. In fact, it is about everyone else but me—and here I was, mystified by someone who did not even work for me or with us. The only thought that played on repeat was: "How did she get us, so clearly and so quickly?"

investisdigital.

Figure I.1   Investis Digital logo.

I also knew the logo was just the beginning. Investis Digital needed a full-scale rebrand and then we needed to roll out the new brand to our global employees and customers. Based on Advantages' precision workflow and ability to capture what we longed to produce, I knew Fran was the right person to help guide and implement the rebrand of Investis Digital.

Though we were just getting to know each other really well, I had a sense that Fran and I were in alignment on our ideas, and while I was curious, I had no idea what I was really getting into. When you are an engineer like me, you think in a linear fashion. Fran's process is circular, from inside out—which is painful to my instinctive linear sensibility. I went along with her in meeting after meeting, however, because if I was going to do this the right way, I knew the effort of learning to understand what she was doing, and why she was doing it, would pay off a hundredfold. Thankfully throughout the process, Fran was patient with my linear sensitivity, and we were able to find a way to communicate the needs of the business.

The Slog

Working through this process with Fran was tedious, but it led to a whole new understanding of the messaging around our logo and the development of the brand foundation for Investis Digital. Just as importantly, for me it was an eye-opening experience. For starters, Fran's process helped our leadership team to understand the components of our brand foundation through the lens of the Three Keys. We defined our purpose, then began defining our values. It was truly a slog. I always believed that values were an important part of running a professional services firm, but I did not really execute on them in the past. Also, I had seen plenty of mission statements calligraphed on boardroom walls that looked amazing but never went any further. Before Fran, we could repeat our values but we were not really living them. With Fran, we wrote our story to share our purpose and values with our teams, clients, and stakeholders.

I believed we would do the same process I had done in the past: get a rebrand, come up with some values, and write them on the conference room wall. Nothing really different. However, working with Fran was different—in all the right ways. From that day forward we had to walk the walk. Fran showed us why there could be no shortcuts, and no substitutions; it had to be about us totally, fully, and completely. And now, having gone through the process, I can tell you one thing: it was worth every moment of the slog. Fran earned my trust by adapting her approach, working at my pace while strategically moving me along in the process when necessary. She never told me the solution—that is not what her framework does. We created clarity around the Three Keys and then infused them throughout all aspects of our global business.

As I went through this slog, I transformed and so did the business, and as a result the value of the process itself became much clearer. Leaders lead by reflecting on what their organization needs; we needed to look different, sound different, and transform into the company we always had the potential to become—and that started with me as CEO.

In general, most people think about service businesses in terms of billable hours. It is far more than that. At its core, the business is about what you stand for—it is about your purpose, values, and story. You need a vision and a pathway to run a successful professional services firm. This is the only way to create a compelling mission that is a rallying cry for your employees. You need to stand for something by creating a lightning rod and being bold enough to stand by it no matter what. Your company needs an identity, and to have an identity in a hypercompetitive global market requires not just leadership, but courage.

As we continued working with Fran, the company's identity went through multiple iterations, honing and refining the Three Keys until they were razor sharp and precise. When we finally had a compelling working set of the Three Keys, we presented them to the team. They were astounded—we had captured who we are and what we believed deep in the core of our ethos, individually and collectively! The team's buy-in was the most important step in the process. Only after going through the Three Keys framework with Fran and articulating the clear purpose, values, and story did I realize how much they were the missing strategic piece in our business. In the past, employees would repeat what they saw on the conference room wall, "Embrace Clarity." Their actions may have implicitly reflected them, but our values were not explicitly documented or communicated. Everyone had it in their heads, but it was not lived day in and day out. They neither knew how to recognize the values in their peers nor how to bring those values forward in relationships with customers. But now, everyone in our global business had structure and a common pattern language around what they were doing and why they were doing it. From coast to coast and across the Atlantic, our global team was ecstatic to move forward with our brand foundation and new identity; a whole new level of engagement had been unleashed. But be forewarned, most organizations do not begin with this level of strategic alignment. However, if you are determined enough as a leader, you will absolutely achieve it.

Since the rebranding, we had made significant progress. For the very first time, our people were really owning and living our values. We saw an immediate impact on the attitudes and engagement of our staff: they yearned to stand for something. We talk about our values in every client pitch, and without a doubt, doing so differentiates us in the marketplace.

Now we look for ways to reinforce our values every day and at specific team-building events. For instance, I host weekly Monday morning "who we are" meetings in the New York office and hold similar meetings when I am in the London or Phoenix offices. I also hold quarterly "connect meetings" in all three offices. We talk about client situations and the current state of the business during the first half of the meeting, then focus on team-building exercises in the second half.

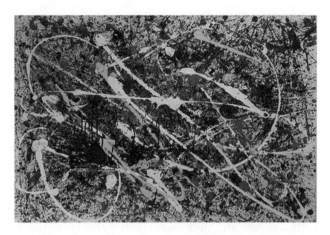

Figure I.2   Investis digital value: Bring Passion.

At one of the London meetings, each team was assigned one of our values and created a piece of modern art to reflect a that value (see Figures I.2, I.3, and I.4). We invited professional artists to our meeting to guide the exercise. We covered the floor with plastic and gave everyone a smock. Paint was flung everywhere, and we had a great time full of laughs and quirky interpretations; our personalities really sprang forth. We then hung the paintings on the wall, reminding each team member that they were a part of creating and reinforcing our values.

Figure I.3   Investis digital value: Embrace Clarity.

Figure I.4   Investis digital value: Inspire Greatness.

Without Fran and her team, we never would have so quickly reached the point where we are living our values daily. And what I learned is just how darn important it is to weave values into everyday interactions and use them as a filter for making remarkable business decisions. But to win in the market, you must first identify your values in order to live them. So let's take a look at Fran's approach and how she developed the comprehensive process.

Finding the Three Keys

In 1992, I (Fran) opened and ran a printing company, but I always spent a lot of time researching and learning about the field of marketing. When a client asked for a price quote for brochures, I'd ask, "Why?" Some clients left us because we had an unconventional approach and I asked too many questions. Those were the transactional-type clients. On the other hand, our really great clients valued my line of questions: "Why do you need this direct-mail piece?" "How will this brochure be used?" "Is this the right collateral to solve your problem?" When the client went down this path with me, typically they did not end up buying what they came for—instead they got what they needed versus what they thought they needed. In the end, I gained a client—not a customer—who bought so much more and valued our relationship, which translated into staying with us for years. I thought I was a good salesperson. I learned over time that part of my success was because I focused on serving the client's needs instead of what they thought they needed. I was a strategist without even strategizing; I just enjoyed asking very particular questions. Our approach was always about the total brand experience—not just the transactional commodity such as a business card, brochure, or a direct mail piece.

For the first few years, I focused on repeatedly asking "why" to our customers in order to distill their "want" down to an actual need, but soon discovered that asking *why* was not enough. I began looking for the other parts of how and where *why* fits into the larger framework of building a brand foundation. After several years of intense trial, error, and iteration within my own dedicated team, I developed a full-circle approach to discovering, designing, and building a brand foundation using the Three Keys to unlock both purpose and profit. We have proven this model over and over since 2005, and the results are nothing less than impressive.

When we worked with Don to rebrand Investis Digital, we laid out the new brand foundation in about thirty days. That is not a typical timeframe. But Don brilliantly led the success of the integration process in the following months. He invested the time to clarify the message with the right words so that he was able to realign his entire team into making an emotional connection to the Three Keys and the brand foundation. Don invested the time with each of his senior leaders to point out the personal alignment and valued contribution they brought to the larger collective company, so they could do the same for the divisions and teams they lead. Everyone began understanding their role in the shared vision. Doing so empowered each leader to lead in a way that makes a personal connection to each of the more than five hundred employees at the company. The reason why everyone loves the brand and is now excited by it is that they can see and feel their personal contribution and value, which fulfills them at a deep, intrinsic level. In Investis Digital, employees are not cogs in a wheel or transactional robots; they are humans who are valued and feel deep purpose in what they do and how they do it, every single day. That is exactly how Don and his board have experienced the direct correlation between a rock-solid brand foundation and rapid productivity, ultimately resulting in increased overall profitability in a condensed timeline.

In *The Business Case for Purpose*, Harvard Business Review Analytics Services reports its findings of a global survey of 474 executives. They write, "Most executives believe purpose matters. 89 percent of executives surveyed said a strong sense of collective purpose drives employee satisfaction; 84 percent said it can affect an organization's ability to transform, and 80 percent said it helps increase customer loyalty."[1]

When a leader has the courage to fully embrace the Three Keys—purpose, values, and story—there will be significant impacts in all aspects of business: sales, marketing, human resources, strategic partnerships, and so on. The Three Keys become the filter through which any leader communicates your brand with employees, vendors, and partners. When you stay aligned with the message, more people will repeat it until they become megaphones for your brand. Ultimately, you begin attracting the right people while simultaneously repelling the wrong people. Your business transforms from shooting crap at a wall to the most powerful, intrinsically motivating magnet humanly possible. This is not opinion, this communications approach is based on neuroscience.

We fully explain the Three Keys—purpose, values, and story—in Chapter 1. Then, chapter by chapter, we walk you through the pieces of leading your professional services firm through the lens of the Three Keys. You can start at the beginning of the book and read through to the end or pick and choose the chapters that address your current needs. In each chapter, you'll learn the principles related to the topic at hand, read our stories, and leave with practical and immediately actionable tasks.

A purposeful brand is built from the inside out, and like any enduring structure it requires a solid foundation. Your brand's foundation is codified in a set of written materials that are authentic, intentional, and customized—the starting point for all brand communication. Let's begin to build yours.

Note

1. https://hbr.org/resources/pdfs/comm/ey/19392HBRReportEY.pdf

1

Create Your Three Keys

Profit is not a purpose, it is a result. To have purpose means the things we do are of real value to others.

—*Simon Sinek,* Start with Why

It is very easy to tell someone what you do. It is far more complex to clearly articulate why you do what you do and, most importantly, why you believe in what you do.

What you will learn in this chapter drives at the core of how to build a successful business. Purpose is the first of the Three Keys that support your brand. Your purpose is why you do what you do, and you must uncover it before you can articulate the values you believe in and the story of who you are. Before you declare what you have to offer the world, explain why it matters.

Correctly defined, purpose captures the essence of your business existence, ultimately driving deep emotional connections with your clients and employees. When both of these synergies occur, as a leader you have a 360-degree feedback loop for any decision you want to make. More tangibly, it is a litmus test for streamlining the entire operation of your company, whether you are a startup venture or an established multinational corporation. Correctly defined purpose ensures that your operations—from the services you offer to the clients you target and accept, the employees you hire, and even the vendors you choose—all match a particular standard and ethos.

At the same time, purpose alone does not form the foundation of your brand. It is only the beginning of the journey. To build a rock-solid foundation, purpose must be combined with comprehensive values and a cohesive story. In this chapter, we'll explore all Three Keys: purpose, values, and story.

Before getting into the Three Keys, let's understand more about what your brand actually is to begin with.

Understand Your Brand Foundation

Every company requires a foundation for all of its communications, both internal and external. If not, communications are ad hoc, uncoordinated, risk confusing the market at large, and immediately commoditize your product or service. This is why the communications foundation must come from the *brand foundation*. Without it, you are just a ship adrift in the middle of the ocean without a compass.

A well-defined brand has two parts:

- Verbal: sets the meaning and messaging for all communications
- Visual: represents the brand visually with logo, color, typefaces, and the like

Companies need to establish the verbal part of the brand before they can begin to design the visual representation. The verbal brand informs the logo. If a business hasn't fully defined and developed their verbal part first, they are planting the seeds of failure. The business might end up with a beautiful design but it will lack meaning. This is one of the reasons why organizations change their logo so often, especially in the early years: a complete lack of strategic clarity.

Don on Fran's Process: "This is why Fran asks her clients deep, fundamental questions about their purpose and values before beginning any visual design work—and ultimately, this is why her logo design and global rebranding for Investis Digital was spot on. The logo was not just a pretty design; it had meaning, and context connected to our purpose, which made it the obvious choice."

Conventional wisdom believes a brand foundation is for external use, mainly marketing (covered in Chapter 6). Many believe the brand foundation is the corporate logo and style guide, with rules about fonts and color. This is only partially right—those things are all parts of branding. But what we are talking about here is comprehensively different. A business does not transform itself from inside out because of a pretty logo and style guide; it takes investment in countless deep conversations, strategic decisions, and the ability of leadership to embrace change for themselves and their business. This is what purpose does: catapult strategic change in order to align all aspects of the business, creating new profitable relationships and collaborations.

For instance, if you got out from behind your desk right this second and asked each employee, "What does our organization mean to you?" the responses would be robotic at best. They would most likely be unable to recite any part of what the company supposedly believes: the vision, mission, purpose, and values. If this is the case in your company, you have some critical strategic work to do. Sure, you may have a guide that articulates your vision, mission, purpose, and values. Most likely if you do, these are all described inside a brand book of sorts. The real question is: "Are you and the rest of your team living them every single day, and using them to inform every single decision?"

The answer: of course not.

Understand the Three Keys

The brand foundation every services business requires to compete in a 21st-century hypercompetitive world is composed of the Three Keys—purpose, values, and story. Done right, these provide the basis of everything you do in your business, and are infused in every communication, process, and internal and external interaction. In order to be strategic, you must place the brand foundation at the center of your business. To begin the process, you have to understand what your firm is all about and why you are even in business. You cannot properly lead an organization, design its structure, execute sales and marketing, or hire the right people without a brand foundation. Literally, you cannot. You might get lucky once or twice, but eventually, your luck will run out and the house of cards will collapse.

With a brand foundation strategically implemented across all aspects of the organization, you can start leading your organization in ways that bring increased productivity and communication, which in turn translate into greater profits. Throughout this book, we show you how the Three Keys eventually emerge in every successful business and provide insight into why and how you should be implementing them into your business, too. The appendix walks you through the process of identifying and defining your purpose, values, and story.

Purpose: The First Key

Purpose is the starting point for an organization, regardless of size. Purpose acts as an anchor that guides everyday decisions and behaviors. You start your brand foundation with your purpose: it becomes the magnet that attracts the right people, partners, and profits while repelling all the wrong ones. A clearly defined purpose improves communication, which ensures increasingly strategic sales and, ultimately, faster closing rates. Purpose is the key to elevating your B-players into A-players, and A-players into the few superstars who drive 80 percent of the business.

Your purpose is the fundamental linchpin for driving the massive change or exponential impact you seek in this world. In "The Business Case for Purpose," the *Harvard Business Review* defined organizational purpose as "an aspirational reason for being which inspires and provides a call to action for an organization and its partners and stakeholders and provides benefit to local and global society."[1] Purpose redefines and focuses the things you do every day to achieve a strategic end result that speaks to your core beliefs. To compete as a professional service company in the 21st century, you need to be able to clearly articulate your purpose. When you do that, the business gains strategic clarity about what it does and whom it is done for, and the end result the leadership expects.

Purpose has three elements:

- Your Why
- A bold vision
- A compelling mission

Why

Looking at the way businesses communicate, we see a clear pattern. Most companies first talk about what they do—the product or service they offer. Next, to some extent, they talk about their How—the differentiators. What they believe makes them different from their competitors. And finally, very few ever get to their Why—their belief, cause, or overall purpose. In his seminal work, *Start with Why*, Simon Sinek identified this as the critical missing piece for building successful companies with compelling offerings.

Great companies start with their purpose, or Why, then move to the How, and finally explain the What. Conventional wisdom is the diametric opposite. Yet, how human beings are hardwired is exactly WHY-HOW-WHAT, not WHAT-HOW-WHY. Since your Why, or purpose, is so critical to your brand foundation and takes the primary role in your communication, it is critical to dig deep to uncover your authentic purpose.

Vision and Mission

Vision and mission are by far two of the most frequently misunderstood business terms. Let's get some quick clarity on the fundamental difference between vision and mission before we dive into how they apply in your business:

- A vision articulates the wide-ranging impact the business will achieve if you and your employees are living your mission well.
- A mission is the rallying cry around what you do consistently, every day, which ultimately achieves your vision.

Said another way:

- A mission is what we execute on every day. As a result, when defining your brand foundation, it is imperative to write your mission in the present tense. A mission identifies your best customers, so keep them in mind when writing. The goal is to identify directly and succinctly what your business does for your best customers, framing the value proposition in a way that shows a valuable contribution.
- On the other hand, a vision is an aspiration that is bigger than the company itself, one that it constantly seeks to live up to. Therefore, when defining your vision, focus on writing in the future tense. For instance, what will the world look like when the business directly impacts every stakeholder you can think of? Think ahead. Dream big. Go beyond the transactional aspects of money.

Here is a perfect example:

- Don's mission and vision for Investis Digital:
  - Mission: To create, amplify, and optimize meaningful communications with audiences across all digital channels
  - Vision: A world where businesses have trusting, meaningful, and enduring relationships with their communities

Your mission and vision are actually two sides of the same leadership coin you hold within yourself. As the leader in your company, the formula could read: If mission, then vision. If HOW, then WHY.

Once you know your company's purpose—why you do what you do—it is time to explore how you will do it.

Values: The Second Key

Values emerge from a completely different place than your purpose. Purpose is limbic and visceral. Values are based on data and psychology. In this ever-changing world, values are constant. They are the immovable object in your life and your business. Values must be unshakeable and unbreakable, under any circumstance, because they drive the moral and ethical compass of the people, places, and profits you will or will not entertain.

Only in the last fifty years or so have businesses begun thinking about intentionally designing their cultures and how the moral and ethical compass of leadership ultimately drives the organization. Values-based organizations are truly purpose-driven, talking about what they believe in, what is important to their stakeholders, and how they perceive the world. Unbreakable values underpin every century-old organization because they provide an actionable framework for operating the company. They act as a filter for strategic decision-making and form a simple tool for analyzing why things went wrong and understanding why things went right across any division of your business. Understanding how to lead a values-based organization sets you distinctly apart from you competition and provides a roadmap for creating a unique value proposition: How do you do business, compared to industry competitors? What does your business promise its clients?

Values are:

- Actionable statements that direct behavior
- The essence of how everyone in your organization does things
- Simple decision-making filters or tools

Values are not:

- Descriptions of the work you do
- Strategies you employ to accomplish the mission
- Competencies, technical or otherwise

There are two types of values, core and shared:

- Core values are individual values developed from your own personal strengths. True core values start with the strengths of the corporate visionary—you! While there are many exercises on the internet that claim to assist you in defining your values, there really is no good shortcut here. You do not want to choose from what other people consider to be values; you want to uncover your existing, authentic values.
- Shared values are created by transforming your core values into business-oriented values or blending the core values of the top-level leadership.

True values-based organizations are also concerned about the value each individual person contributes. The age-old saying is true, one bad apple spoils the whole bunch. It is easy to forget in the craziness of our daily lives how it is the sum of the parts, together, that ensures the company runs smoothly. When leadership achieves cohesion and unity among all employees, the business gains waves of cascading momentum to achieve rapid revenue growth and exponential impact. This is how people become excited to come to work every day—they feel safe, valued, and deeply invested in accomplishing the defined mission. As a result, they become more productive, more engaged, and synchronized in greater unison toward your organization's compelling vision.

To give you an example, the shared values at Fran's company, Advantages, are:

- Be Tenacious
- Earn Trust
- Be Process Oriented

- Be the Sherpa
- Aspire Higher

You can view a graphic interpretation that hangs on the conference room wall in Figure 1.1.

Shared values done right should be at the forefront of everything your company does: as soon as a client walks in the door, and at the beginning of every presentation. This is what shared values look like: when every single employee is able to clearly explain how they are guided to do things in the business, because your shared values translate into direct decision-making and behavior. Values inspire and empower employees and clearly compel or repel clients. When you truly explain and demonstrate values, everyone in the company becomes aligned, and clients learn to know what to always expect from your business. Values guide the business by clarifying, internally and externally, who you are and what you stand for. They will also attract good "fits"—employees, customers, vendors—and repel those who do not share the same values.

Once you have these values, repeat them constantly—live and breathe them, day in and day out, 24/7, 365. When you commit to

Figure 1.1   Advantages' values on display.

doing that, a values-based culture emerges, creating a predictable and trustworthy culture as well as complete control of the business's brand narrative.

One of Don's Values for Investis Digital
Embrace Clarity

For Investis Digital, this value is demonstrated internally and externally by using plain language to communicate clearly how we solve problems and by taking the time to explain in simple terms what we do and how we do it—that's how we build trust.

At Fran's suggestion, we identified a famous quote that brings it together:

"Simplicity is the ultimate sophistication."
—*Leonardo da Vinci*

Shared values are actionable and most stem from the organic ethos and nature of the company itself. Investis Digital was started twenty years ago in the investor relations space. The investor relations audience wants clear and to-the-point communication; tell it like it is and nothing more. As the company grows and expanded its offerings, that characteristic permeated everything we do. Embrace Clarity is a value that has held true since our beginnings, but it is articulated more clearly today.

When a business scales quickly or encounters missteps, most leaders stop thinking about their brand foundation as the cornerstone. At one point, they decided to write their vision and mission statements to communicate their purpose, identified and named their values, and then they went back to business as usual believing the work was complete. Values are not written; they are lived. After you have determined your Why and uncovered and articulated your values, we turn to the third key: Story. Story provides the visualization for values that creates emotion and develops deep connection, collaboration, and communication with your internal and external customers.

Story: The Third Key

Storytelling is the fundamental tool of human experience-sharing. Stories resonate with people much more than ice-cold data or bland XY graphs. Good stories create emotional connections between the reader and the subject. They strategically support your message when marketing and selling your company to potential employees and clients. When written in an engaging format, stories are magnets that attract people like you and—the bonus—repel bad fits. See the trend? Every aspect of the Three Keys creates a fundamental magnet that breeds communication, collaboration, and; connection while simultaneously attracting the right people, partners, and profits—and repelling the rest.

Your brand reputation has never been so important, and story is how you develop, institutionalize, and maintain it. In this age of fake news, where the public is plagued by untruths, overburdened with information, and remains skeptical of what they hear and read, leaders must own and protect the stories of their company. The fact is, in the 21st century, if your business isn't telling and owning its own story, someone else will take control of the narrative. Think about that for a minute.

What's more, with all the static being spewed out by countless media outlets, businesses compete for the public's overwhelmed and limited attention span. Your purpose and values differentiate your firm from others, and your story is the opportunity to weave your Three Keys together in a compelling manner that creates the emotional connections with the people who align with you. A successful story informs others who you are, what you believe in, and why what you are doing is important to like-minded believers. The story controls the brand narrative and provides relevance and connection. As Maya Angelou once said, "People will forget what you said, people will forget what you did,

Figure 1.2   A piece of Advantages' origin story.

but people will never forget how you made them feel." Storytelling is organic; it directly connects to what Fran calls "story-doing," defined as authentically living the brand's purpose through its actionable values. Done right, this leads to "story-sharing," when others retell your stories, thereby amplifying your authentic brand. Storytelling becomes story-doing, which becomes story-sharing, a true tribal megaphone by a ministry who believes what you believe. Your story can be told in words and images. In Figure 1.2, you can see a piece of the Advantages' origin story that hangs on the wall in the office.

The Investis Digital Origin Story

In the process of rebranding the merged companies Investis and ZOG Digital to become Investis Digital, the story told to the market had to be crafted. Investis Digital wasn't either of the predecessor companies; it was something different, something better. Better because of the combination. Better because the core values of the individual leaders evolved into the shared values of the new entity. Whereas Investis previously serviced the corporate sector by delivering investor relations information to shareholders, the new company creates, optimizes, and amplifies meaningful communication to audiences across all digital channels. In today's hyper-connected, always-on world, honest communication has never been more important or reputation more fragile. Purpose and narrative matter: what companies say about themselves and what others say about them matters more than ever before. At the same time, businesses often struggle to create a compelling brand narrative and share it consistently across multiple digital platforms. We help corporations build relationships with their stakeholders across boundaries, cultures, and borders. The new company offered the unique value proposition of both digital performance marketing and investor communications. This platform served as the basis for creating a fast-growing business offering, a service previously unavailable to the global market and a new company.

Apply the Three Keys to Your Business

You know what you do, whether it is building widgets or offering consulting services. You know how you do it and you may even believe that how you build your widget or the consulting method you use differentiates you from the competition. The truth is, *why* you do what you do—your cause, purpose, and belief living at the center of how and what you do—is the differentiator. To be effective, you must clearly articulate the purpose, values, and story behind your company and weave them into everything you and your employees do internally and externally.

When speaking to employees, clients, customers, or stakeholders, the conventional wisdom is to discuss everything "from the outside in," talking first about the product or service you sell, yet there are dozens, if not hundreds of other businesses doing the same. What if, instead, you align around a common goal and use it as a direct way to connect with anyone associated with your business? Outcome: you begin to create a long-term relationship built, first and foremost, on trust. An added benefit of leading a values-based firm is the ability to pivot as clients or the market demand other offerings, all while standing steadfast in your values and purpose. A values-based firm is more agile because it has trusted relationships with clients rather than transactions. There is a sense of conviction of quality. With deep relationships, it doesn't matter what you are selling today or tomorrow; clients stay with you because they trust you and are convinced you will always have their back, no matter what you do.

Are You a Values-Based, Purpose-Driven Firm?

If you don't know your purpose, values, and story, it's time to figure them out—right now. If they are just lifeless words on a conference room wall, it is time to stop paying them lip service. Start intentionally designing the way forward for your business and all its stakeholders.

Truth be told, it is not easy to articulate the world you want to see. To boil it down into a succinct, beautiful purpose statement takes many reflective hours of investment. Clearly identifying your values is absolutely a slog, and writing your story is certainly challenging. Yet these Three Keys are the most critical linchpin to the success of your business, in a world of saturated markets. Clients and employees thirst for an engaged relationship based on shared beliefs more than on a low price or a high salary.

Every individual company and leader lives and breathes their values differently, and it is those values that inform organizational culture. Understand that this process is about finding your own rhythm and activating the values that matter most. You need to make an investment in your people and their connectedness by becoming consistently clear and available. Regardless of your communication style, an interesting thing happens when everyone in the organization understands where the company's going and what it stands for—employees and clients become enthusiastic fans who share your story, allowing you to scale your firm faster and with more agility as you outpace your competition. You are also going to sleep better at night!

What Can You Do Now?

While you want to consider your purpose, values, and story comprehensively, you might not have the time or budget for an immediate, full-stack overhaul. There are some quick, short-term changes you can implement in the meantime:

- Revisit your tagline. In five words or fewer, distinctively tell the world why you do what you do—and make those words actionable.
- Rethink your business card. While many believe business cards are obsolete, in the professional services arena we still rely on that little card to remind people who we are and what we do; make sure yours reflect your purpose and showcase your memorable brand personality. If your business card doesn't stand out from the pack, you will end up in the pile that has rubber bands around it in a desk drawer. (You know the ones I'm talking about—the old ones from last year's networking event. The rubber band breaks, you sift through the cards, and discard 90 percent of them because you can't remember who the person is.) Make sure yours stands out!
- Make your digital footprint reinforce your brand. The brand foundation should reveal itself in each and every communication you exchange with your clients and employees—from your email signature to LinkedIn profiles—and it costs next to nothing. Make sure the same template is shared with anyone who signs their name with your domain.
- Lead with your three Keys. Greet with your brand first. For example, state your purposeful tagline when you answer the phone at work.
- Infuse your Three Keys into everything you do. The remaining chapters of the book show you how to ensure that the Three Keys drive the decisions you make and the actions you take as the leader of a professional services firm.

As you'll see in the next chapter, culture is the essence of any organization and cannot be left to run itself.

Like your brand—to which it is so closely tied—either you define the culture, or it defines you. Either it grows with you or constricts you. If you've founded a start-up, you have a blank slate to work with and don't have obstacles in your way to set the tone. If you are a leader of an established organization, you already have a defined culture. Either way, with the proper time investment and resources, you have the opportunity to either define or redefine your culture. If you don't like what you have, step up and make the changes needed to reshape your culture—remember the great results Don saw after going through the slog?

The Three Keys are the tools to make transformational change happen, although establishing your Three Keys will not happen overnight, and it will take more than just you and your own brain. To achieve long-term sustainable success, you will need to lead this effort by continuing to motivate and educate the next generation of leadership, so they can build upon it. Our purpose is to help you better lead the service organization you are a part of today by taking advantage of all Three Keys. Because once you do, greater people, partners, and profits will inevitably follow. We know because we are living examples of the process and have been reaping its rewards for years.

Now that we have aligned the beginning of your brand foundation, it is time to move up a level, starting with your company culture. Here we will begin to look at how to incorporate your purpose, values, and story into every aspect of your business in order to unlock powerful purpose and unrealized profit.

Notes

1. https://www.ey.com/Publication/vwLUAssets/ey-the-business-case-for-purpose/$FILE/ey-the-business-case-for-purpose.pdf

2

Values–Based Culture

Company culture is the product of a company's values, expectations, and environment.
   —*Courtney Chapman, product manager, Rubicon Project*

Culture is more powerful than any law, belief system, knowledge, or process. Professional services firms today face challenges that didn't exist twenty or thirty years ago. The way we work has changed: organizations used to be housed under one roof and everyone worked the same hours. Today, we have the gig economy with remote workers, flex-time workers, 1099s, and multiple generations from babyboomers to Gens X, Y, and Z, with modern demands and desires. Culture is the glue that holds a diverse organization together. To attract top talent and inspire employees to thrive, leaders must adjust their cultures to meet the standards of current and coming generations. Culture helps to create the new markets, experiences, products, services, content, or processes necessary for a company to survive and grow.

The Three Keys—your purpose, values, and story—are the underlying drivers of your culture.

By 2020, millennials will comprise half of the workforce, and Gen Zers will begin entering the workplace. Our corporate cultures must evolve in order to ensure that our organizations have the vital lifeblood, broad knowledge, and increasing momentum to scale creatively, rapidly, and adaptively in the 21st century. The contemporary generations demand that company cultures be more social, free, equal, diversified, and purposeful. A culture that supports a wide range of diversity is as important as the brand, product, service, or the work itself. These cultural qualities are an instrumental means of enticing and retaining talent and effectively increasing the engagement and productivity of current employees.

Culture has always been important, but never to the extent it is today. For some time now, *culture* has been one of the most important words in corporate boardrooms, and for good reason—but that culture must align with your purpose and values and be communicated through your story. You can make every change in the world, follow every best practice, hire the most talented teams, and develop the perfect roadmap for success, but without a culture that's aligned with your Three Keys, none of that will matter.

As the modern workplace evolves, culture has taken an increasingly central role, and that role will only continue to grow. Aine Cain wrote an article for *Business Insider*[1] that provides a historical view of how show business culture has evolved from the 1950s to 2018. She cites several changes in the workplace that reflect the changes we've experienced in society and the world as a whole, including changes in the physical workplace and increased diversity in the workforce. As these changes continue to reshape and restructure both how we work and the meaning of work, leaders must place an increased emphasis on the development of a shared culture in place of a more traditional culture based upon a division between commanding bosses and obedient employees.

Culture norms continually evolve, but that evolutionary velocity hit overdrive around 2000. The business world struggles to catch up and embrace this new normal. Many companies give lip service to the impact of culture on organizations while others are putting their money where their mouths are. It is one thing for an organization to slap buzzwords such as *collaboration*, *egalitarianism*, and *teamwork* on its conference room walls and website. It is another thing entirely to run a business based on such principles. If you don't take your values seriously, your customers and stakeholders won't take them—or you— seriously, either; they'll take their business to another firm that stands by and lives the values they claim. To succeed in the 21st century and beyond, professional services companies must establish values as the way they do business and as the filter through which all decisions are made.

Three Building Blocks of Culture

Culture comprises the values, beliefs, behaviors, artifacts, and reward systems that influence people's behavior on a day-to-day basis. Culture is values in action, and top leadership drives the health of company culture through everyday processes and behaviors.

Culture is built on three principles:

1. Leadership owns culture.
2. Culture is pervasive.
3. Communicate your culture.

Let's take a closer look at the three building blocks as the foundation for designing a culture built to thrive in the 21st century.

Leadership Owns Culture

An organization's culture lives and dies with the visionary leader— the CEO—who influences the culture within the organization by articulating and embedding values, hiring and growing talent, and aligning organizational systems. The leader's values define and drive the organization's culture. You need to walk the walk in the area of values more than in any other aspect of your business. If you're not behaving in a way that reflects your values, no one else will, either.

The world's most successful CEOs agree that the most important thing they do is shape and reinforce the organization's culture. CEOs need to develop and embed values that reflect flexibility, initiative, and adaptability inside their organizations so that they are prepared to respond to disruptions in their business environments.

A strong, unified culture must:

- Positively contribute to image, values, brand, and identity
- Help to determine and achieve goals
- Attract and retain increasingly better talent
- Attract and retain aligned customers

Our job as leaders is to consistently live our values because they create a framework for everyone—internal and external—to connect to. As Bob Leduc, president of aerospace powerhouse Pratt & Whitney, said "I am a firm believer that my job is to define the culture we want, model the culture we want, and nourish the culture we want."

Establish Boundaries

Don came into Investis US during very uncertain times. Despite lagging profits in U.S. operations, a rather free-spirited culture existed in the New York office, led by a manager who had transferred over from London. Don tells the story:

It immediately became clear to me that the managing director liked to party. I do not want to sound like the old fuddy-duddy. I want a team that bonds and enjoys each other's company, but not primarily using company-sponsored happy hours that last late into the night. That's not the team-building, family atmosphere I imagined for Investis Digital.

Even after that free-wheeling managing director left, the happy hour mentality remained. People looked forward to going out together after work. I was glad they got along and wanted to be in one another's company. But the few times I joined them, I found they stayed at the bar a lot longer than I expected. I wondered how they got to work the next day. I set out to gently yet firmly change company culture.

I like having fun, but there are limits. I have had a personal rule throughout my career: no matter what the work event, I never stay past about 10:00 p.m., because nothing positive happens after that hour. Plus, I like my job too much to feel groggy in the morning from staying out late the night before. I didn't want to be the leader in the ivory tower, so I joined in the happy hours, but at the next party I started saying my goodbyes around 8:30 p.m., and as I headed out the door I said, "Enjoy yourselves, but I look forward to seeing you all bright and early in the morning." Then I left.

This was my mantra at all the happy hours, close the tab early—yes, the company was paying—and lead by example. At first, a few people would still step over the line and get a little tipsy or do something inappropriate. The next day I would raise an eyebrow as I heard the gossip. "You should have seen Sam last night." Well, you can bet I'm going to walk by and ask Sam how he is feeling. If you do that enough, Sam gets the idea that his behavior may be inappropriate. Little by little, the party atmosphere slowed down, and now it's in line with the overall culture being cultivated at the firm.

Everyone here knows what I stand for, and more importantly, why. A few months ago, I went to a happy hour and as the event was wrapping up at 9 p.m., someone said, "Time to go, right, Don?" And I left the restaurant pleased that my consistent actions had been noticed.

Your leadership team, employees, clients, and partners all need to know what you stand for and why. The saying "Actions speak louder than words" could not be truer than when it comes to demonstrating the values that you want to instill in your culture.

Culture Is Pervasive

Culture is for everyone. One definition of culture is the way that anyone within the "group" acts or performs. For a values-based culture to be effective, it needs to start with the leader and flow down. Culture must be pervasive, affecting everyone in the organization, from top to bottom and across all silos.

When your leadership team and employees operate from the same values, they are implicitly in agreement on the culture, and you will have a far easier time getting buy-in across the organization. Culture is memetic; when one or two employees emulate your behavior, other employees will emulate them, and the culture will pervade the entire organization. An organization that has a cohesive culture isn't distracted by petty disagreements. Employees with a shared culture work together toward a common defined purpose, which has a direct impact on your profits.

Likewise, if one person is out of sync with the culture, their behavior can disrupt the flow and function of the entire team. You can easily spot the troublemakers. They're the people who come in late, leave early, embellish their expense reports, and always have excuses. You come to realize the train isn't late every day, they are. Their negativity and poor behavior lead to resentment from your other aligned team members.

One of the benefits of a strong, pervasive culture is that it organically weeds out those who aren't ethically aligned with your organization. If they don't self-select out, however, you need to cut them. People who are a bad culture fit do irreparable harm to your culture, and chances are they are better suited for a job someplace else.

Communicate Your Culture

Clear communication is the core pillar of any good relationship. To develop a values-based culture, you need to communicate clearly what those values are and reinforce them repeatedly.

Communication is more than what you explicitly say; it's what you communicate through the ways you act, react, reward, and reprimand. Think purposefully about your "silent communication" of values. If one of your values relates to respecting others' time, and you consistently arrive late, you are speaking volumes about how you feel about that value without ever saying a word.

Communication is not preaching; it's a highly dynamic two-way street. Your teams are what make your culture great. Listen to how they communicate —both verbally and nonverbally—with you and others within and outside the organization. Active listening provides the best metric of where your teams stand in relation to values, where they struggle to maintain those values, and how you can best lead them to better live your values-based culture.

Communication Builds Culture and Teams

Leaders must tell people what they stand for and lead by example. Aligning your words and actions shows that you mean what you say and say what you mean. Reinforcing core values in the company culture is a combination of communication and team-building exercises. Communicate and do it frequently!

You probably already communicate with your team members in various ways, such as through email or performance reviews. But those traditional ways do not provide enough opportunities for employees to truly open up and completely buy into the culture. Take advantage of current trends and opportunities to host town hall meetings or develop an in-house podcast. Here are a few suggestions for communicating that offer an opportunity to reinforce the culture you want to see in your organization.

- Don releases a weekly newsletter called "Don's Download." This is an opportunity to celebrate company-wide accomplishments and more deeply explain and celebrate the role and power of our values. It's the only communication that goes out to the whole company to ensure that the same culture exists in New York as it does in London and Phoenix or anywhere else in the world.
- Weekly meetings are common in professional services organizations, but Fran does them differently. She holds a fifteen-minute standing meeting every Friday, which she opens by stating the company's mission and vision. Every team member comes prepared to talk about what didn't go well that week, seeking to identify places where those slipups or errors were linked to a misalignment with company values. It's not about pointing fingers; it's about addressing issues head on and learning to improve. Meetings end on a positive note by sharing accolades received from clients and giving a shout-out to anyone who has demonstrated organizational values in an exemplary way during the week.
- Consider using the first half of longer quarterly meetings to talk about client situations and the state of the business, then focus on team-building exercises in the second half.
- Fran suggests finding a quote from a famous person to represent each of your values. For example, one of her company's values is to "bring passion." A Friedrich Hegel quote, "Nothing great in the world was accomplished without passion," reminds everyone that their passion should be visible in every service they provide. Quotes should be displayed where team members will see them often, such as on stands that rest on conference room tables or desks.

People will accept and align with the values and culture over time, but it all comes back to how much you communicate and live them, and how passionately you do so. There are tactical things you can do to build culture:

1. Cultivate employee relationships. Allow employees time to get to know each other. Build community through small group dinners or an outing to a sporting or cultural event.
2. Invest in employee perks that resonate with both your values and your employees. Engage your team and casually ask them which possible benefits they prefer. Some organizations host company happy hours while others offer wellness programs and free snacks.
3. Appropriately reward employees for good performance. Rewards should align with your culture and be meaningful and make a personal connection to the employee. Some employees may value a day off with pay while others will be pleasantly surprised by a gift card or basket.
4. Be mindful of burnout. Be flexible and understanding with employees, especially during times when their workload is high.

As we said at the beginning of this chapter, the success of a professional service company begins with culture. When a company's culture is clearly aligned with business strategy, it attracts people who feel comfortable in it, producing a high level of engagement, which in turn leads to profitability. Both culture and engagement require CEO and C-suite commitment and strong support from HR to understand, measure, and improve.

Keep Remote Workers Involved

Remote workers present their own set of distinct challenges when it comes to communicating and sustaining culture. In a professional services firm, you may also have employees who spend more time at the client site than in your office, who share many of the same challenges that remote workers face. Don asked Taylor Billings Seitz, Director of Client Services in the United States for Investis Digital, to share some tips to make sure remote workers are not only aware of your organization's culture but also feel that they are part of it. We've summarized Billings Seitz's advice here.

Remote workers often miss out on day-to-day details and exchanges that reinforce company culture. They feel isolated and lack the camaraderie of a team. They may do their job well but feel like no one notices. They may be afraid to talk to a manager or colleagues about issues because their remote situation could be blamed as the cause.

It's the leader or manager's responsibility to establish and maintain an open line of communication with remote workers. To that end, the leader must:

- Be approachable and reachable. This can be via email, phone, virtual videoconference, and so on.
- Make sure employees know there is never a situation "too scary" or "too little" to ask about.
- Employees should be encouraged to solve issues on their own, but not hide those issues from their managers.
- Provide top-down communications. Talk openly about personnel decisions, company decisions, and other issues.
- Offer employees scheduled opportunities for communication.

Use technology to keep remote workers informed and involved. Hold videoconference calls on a regular basis so the remote workers and the onsite team can put a face and voice to the signature on the email. Bringing remote workers to the office at least once a quarter for team-building exercises breaks down barriers and reinforces camaraderie.

Respond to the Millennial Workforce

Studies show that millennial professionals are more selective about the organizations they work with, considering not just the job itself and its associated benefits but especially company values. Millennials are not looking only for a paycheck—they want to work for companies that distinctly and definitively align with their personal beliefs and core values.

In addition to seeking shared values, recent research[2] has shown that millennials are idealistic and flock to companies that value and practice inclusivity. They desire a healthy work–life balance and the opportunity for personal growth. They seek positions that offer a sense of purpose, meaning, and fulfillment. A study from Deloitte reports, "Two out of three millennials state their organization's purpose is the reason they choose to work there, yet only one out of five millennials in organizational cultures without perceived purposes is satisfied with their work."[3]

Millennials want to make an impact both on and off the job. They want to volunteer and make a difference with their co-workers, as opposed to volunteering on a solo basis. They also want to know how their work impacts society. Look for ways to give them the opportunities to make an impact, and then celebrate them when they succeed.

Millennials and Investis Digital

As has been stated, today's young professionals make decisions about their work with a different lens than used in the past. In order to address the needs of this generation, frameworks and structures within organizations need to reflect their purpose-driven desires. In creating Investis Digital's culture, the focus on the Three Keys has been critical to developing an inclusive work environment that is attractive to younger workers and conducive to delivering the best work possible. This is all about communication. Both internally and externally, as a firm, we must embrace our values, even celebrate them—millennials want to see the Three Keys in action every day.

Innovate and Evolve Culture

So, what does all this mean when it comes to leading a professional services organization?

Innovation is the lifeblood of growth. If a company is going to continue on a growth path, it has to be constantly innovating. Recent research[4] published by Accenture sheds some light on culture and its direct influence on innovation within professional services firms, large or small. Accenture defines innovative employees as purposeful, collaborative, free, and inspired team members who quickly form new ideas they are not afraid to share. Successful company cultures build innovative employees through autonomy, trust, equal treatment, and equal opportunity to grow.

Accenture's findings focus on creating a culture of equality that responds neatly to the desires of today's millennial workforce. A culture of equality—meaning a workplace environment that helps everyone advance to higher positions—is a powerful multiplier of innovation and growth. When you consider that personal growth is important to millennial professionals, a clear growth path in the organizational structure responds to their needs.

Investis Digital's Multigenerational Culture

Investis Digital employs people of all ages. Don shares a story about making sure all of them are valued for their contribution:

We have a music server that pipes music throughout the office. We encouraged employees to add songs they like to the playlist. One woman in her sixties loaded the playlist with songs from the seventies, dominating the space with her music choice. The twenty-somethings in the office started to complain that they wanted to hear more current music. Rather than turn the situation into a human resources issue, everyone participated in an office-wide project. We all contributed our individual playlists of songs and put them on our music server. We limited the number of songs any one person can add to the playlist. We also purchased headphones for anyone who didn't want to listen to the office music, so that they could listen to their personal music choices. Six people opted for headphones while the others felt more involved in the music choice on the office playlist.

Create a Culture of YES!

Big risky projects are scary and full of challenges. Many firms have a tendency to shy away from daunting programs that seem at the outset to be out of reach. However, when your organization is internally aligned on a purpose that your client shares, say, "Yes!" No matter how daunting the project is, you will be able to collect the resources you need and solve any problems that arise. This is a chance to expand your teams' capabilities and get out of your comfort zone. Great opportunities don't present themselves every day, so create a culture of "yes" and embrace every purposeful challenge that comes your way.

Fran Says, "YES!"

Fran tells a story of when she said, "YES!" and the impact it had on her business and team:

A few years back, the VP of business development at Rupert Murdoch's education company Amplify (née Wireless Generation), asked me to review a 60-page printing bid for cutting edge learning assets. Amplify wanted to drive change across the educational publishing business. I told the VP the company's approach was all wrong, and that they would overspend by millions if they didn't change their approach. He invited me to a meeting two days later to discuss the project.

(continued)

I'd never seen a boardroom that size. Murdoch's education czar sat at the head of the table, presiding over close to three dozen people. The discussion went around the table until the CEO stood up and said, "Goddammit, can somebody just tell me how we're going to beat our competitors in this market because I'm not leaving this room until that happens."

I raised my hand and said, "If you want to beat your competitors in a bloated market and do it within six months, you have to take an entrepreneurial approach. You have to break all your silos. And as an entrepreneur myself, I will lead the project and get you to market and miles ahead of everyone else." Everyone looked at me. He pointed at me as he stood to go and said, "You're hired. Go figure it out."

I had no idea what I'd just said yes to except that I had a strong plan to break the vicious cycle in which they were already engaged. I didn't know who many of these people were or what "silos" existed, but all of a sudden, I was in charge of a project—and I didn't even work directly for the company. I knew this was an opportunity of a lifetime, and I wasn't going to fail. The head of business development, who became a friend of mine, walked in, closed the office door, and said, "What the f#*k did you just do?"

I said, "I don't know everything right now, but we're going to figure it out. YES, we can do this. YES, we have the right resources and the right talent. YES, we will succeed and do so with panache."

It took me under a week to get my sea legs out from under me, but we figured out how to deliver doing so in "chunks." It would be foolish to think we could produce a year of content in months. So what did we do? We delivered in a "just-in-time" method approach. We produced a hundred days of content at a time. I locked arms with the head of our art department to tackle this monumental project, regularly reviewing the spreadsheet I'd built to represent all the components of the project—the columns reaching double Z. I staffed up three 24/7 shifts to create 168 InDesign components. I purchased close to a dozen computers and filled the seats in front of them in less than three days.

Throughout the hectic process, I consistently reminded my team of our company vision and our collective desire to always "Aspire Higher." I framed this challenge as an opportunity that would help us get there. We met all the deadlines for this project and continued to deliver for the company for three additional years—because I recognized the power behind a confident team with a culture of "YES!

Culture and the Three Keys

The components of each of the Three Keys help leaders achieve a unified culture. Remember, purpose (the first key) can be defined as the things you do every day to get to the end results that speak to your core belief. Purpose is comprised of your mission, which allows the organization to better understand what they are committed to each and every day, and your vision, which keeps everyone's attention on where they are going. Your culture comes through in everything you do to support your purpose.

Values (the second key) are culture in action. Values underpin the whole organization and provide the actionable framework from which you run your company. Values also serve as a filter for making better, more informed decisions and a clear perspective for analyzing why something may have gone wrong. The link between values and culture can be particularly useful when someone isn't living up to the organization's culture; you can look to your values to determine why the person isn't in alignment.

Your story (the third key) informs others who you are as a business, what you believe in, and why you matter to them, specifically.

Your culture is reflected in the story your brand narrative tells and provides relevance and connection. This is an opportunity to demonstrate your culture to those outside your organization as well as those within.

The leader who embodies the organization's culture is much more than just one step ahead of the game. As Jon Katzenbach and DeAnne Aguirre write in *Strategy+Business* magazine:[5]

> If you are the chief executive of a company that is sailing with the wind and leading in its competitive race, that's a sign that your culture is in sync with your strategy. This makes your company much more likely to deliver consistent and attractive profitability and growth results. You can tell you have such a culture because people are confident and energized. They can justifiably take pride in the results of their work. As CEO, your role is to keep the ship on course and ahead of the competition. This requires generating regular behavioral reminders about the values, aspirations, and engagements that underlie your company's success and reinforce its strategy.

What Can You Do?

To create a strong and deeply interconnected culture of trust, respect, and autonomy, start by developing your company values. Then allow those values to determine the actions and strategies that reinforce the culture. Remember, first and foremost, the purpose and values of the culture and company must be in alignment. Once your culture is defined, you want it to permeate the entire organization; your goals should be to:

- Empower others: Coach your staff. Strive not only to embody and cultivate the culture, but also guide others and offer support on their path.
- Implement value-based hiring: Value-based hiring focuses on identifying how well a candidate's beliefs, passions, and competencies align with the organization's values during the hiring process.

- Build community: Break down department divides to bring employees together and cultivate creativity.

In the next few chapters, we will dive significantly deeper into these three points by focusing on how to lead, hire, and structure your organization. When you have stepped up as a leader to build or reshape a values-based culture that is clearly communicated and lived throughout the organization, you will have established a culture that is built to last. A sustainable values-based culture means that you have so much acceptance and saturation that it becomes part of the very fabric of the organization. That's the type of culture that lives on beyond the tenure of even the greatest leader.

Notes

1. https://www.businessinsider.com/office-culture-then-and-now-2018-5
2. https://www.forbes.com/sites/larryalton/2017/06/20/how-millennials-are-reshaping-whats-important-in-corporate-culture-#41f9c6282dfb
3. https://www2.deloitte.com/content/dam/Deloitte/us/Documents/about-deloitte/us-millennial-majority-will-transform-your-culture.pdf
4. https://www.accenture.com/us-en/about/inclusion-diversity/gender-equality-innovation-research?c=acn_glb_gettingtoequalrgoogle_10903764&n=psgs_0319&gclid=EAIaIQobChMI1c2L1Imo4wIViIvICh2cIwoQEAAYASAAEgJlU_D_BwE
5. https://www.strategy-business.com/article/00179?gko=0fb40

3 | Leadership

Leadership is the capacity to influence others through inspiration motivated by passion, generated by vision, produced by a conviction, ignited by purpose.
—*Myles Munroe,* Power of Character in Leadership: How Values, Morals, Ethics, and Principles Affect Leaders

Leadership is more critically important in today's professional services companies than it has ever been. Yet professional service firms struggle in this aspect more than any other type of business. Why? Because leadership can only happen once the proper foundation is established.

In a professional services firm with a strong brand foundation, leaders inspire their teams with purpose, values, and story. In Chapter 2, we discussed how leaders begin their business transformation through culture. Now we are going to explore how leaders infuse their leadership style with the Three Keys so they can inspire their teams to achieve a common goal.

What Is Leadership?

- How can I effectively lead others to success?
- How do I identify future leaders?
- How are values tied to me as a leader?

Webster defines leadership as "the act or instance to direct on a course or in a direction." Legendary management consultant Peter Drucker was blunt in "Your Leadership Is Unique"[1] when he wrote, "Leadership, then, is a process of social influence that maximizes the efforts of others toward the achievement of a goal. It has nothing to do with seniority or one's position or title in the hierarchy of a company, nor personal attributes." Additionally, as John Kotter wrote in *Leading Change,*[2] "One of the key distinctions in business is to understand the difference between leadership and management." On the surface, these two concepts can be easily confused. To quote Drucker again, "Management is about doing things right; leadership is doing the right things."

Although managing people is still vitally important in professional services, it's time to shift perspective and recognize the obligation to lead and grow people. Over the past few decades, the media has been starstruck by the all-encompassing gravitas of legendary CEOs, those who dictated the conversation. But the environment today is different: while the CEO is still centerstage for interactions with markets, a greater emphasis is now placed on overall team dynamics. The world wants to understand the company, its employees, and how they interact to drive value. They are less interested in pontificating CEOs who only want to hear themselves talk. In fact, the greatest credit is given to the leader who can grow and get the best out of their people by molding them into a cohesive executive unit (discussed further in Chapter 4).

Our traditional view of management is task-based and mechanical. Managers constructively delegate, counsel, evaluate, forecast, budget, plan, and control—micromanagement. An article in Forbes[3] identified five ways management and leadership differ:

- A manager oversees a mechanical process while a leader inspires a group to complete a purposeful mission.
- Leaders develop self-awareness and continuously reevaluate their performance and admit when they make mistakes.
- Leaders allow others to lead, inspiring through trust, not fear and hierarchy.
- The leader learns along with the team through collaboration.
- Managers learn procedures and time management—still important skills to have—but leaders learn to deliver messages.

To stay relevant in the 21st century, leaders are responsible for building relationships, and inspiring their workforce through purpose, charisma, and empowerment. Leadership today, as Robert Greenleaf said in his book *Servant Leadership*, is "about service to others and a commitment to developing more servants as leaders. It involves co-creation of a commitment to a mission." Leadership for the 21st century is not about getting employees to do what you say. It's about inspiring employees to work collaboratively and consciously toward a common goal. This is the standard professional services firms need to achieve today.

How do leaders inspire their teams? With the Three Keys: purpose, values, and story. Leaders begin with the culture, as we saw in Chapter 2. Here we look at how leaders infuse their leadership with the Three Keys to inspire teams toward that common goal.

Leading in the 21st Century

Changes in the workplace mirror broad changes in our collective culture. Workplace changes have also accelerated the need for leaders with leadership experience instead of managers with management skills. As professional service firms move away from an autocratic, hierarchical organization charts, management is not the only place where decisions are now being made. When leadership is done right, leaders provide direction, motivation, and continued support to a community of trusted employees who are empowered to make proactive decisions for the business. Teams become empowered by leaders when there is direct alignment and embodiment of the company's purpose, values, and story.

Disruptive technological change also directly impacts every single aspect of an organization. Because of ubiquitous information technology, communication now has the opportunity to be collaborative and transparent, as well as immediate. Therefore, employees exceedingly expect leaders to participate in conversations while also being open and transparent about company performance and the necessary next steps to achieve its vision.

Leadership always evolves, which is reflected by changes in business practices and the emerging cultural values of modern generations. Leaders who lead with emotional intelligence have the ability to capitalize on emerging cultural, interpersonal, and leadership trends by connecting intentionally to inspire those they lead. Deep visceral employee motivation is a direct result of an employee's personal alignment with company values and purpose. Values and purpose are far more substantive and lasting to human beings than command-and-control directives from an egocentric leader who believes compensation is all that matters. While these best practices have always been true of great leaders, in today's professional service workplace, teams expect this behavior as standard operating procedure from their leadership.

Leading an organization today is different than even just twenty years ago. Back then, it was all about the optics. Here was the mindset of the time:

- How early can you get in?
- How late can you stay and be seen?
- What suit are you wearing?
- How close is your office to the boss?
- Most importantly, how big is your office compared to your peers?

Acceptable behavior at that time was to speak when spoken to, especially around the CEO, and when you did speak, sound smart. Other than that, you were not to speak and were to sit quietly in your cubicle.

Times have changed. The days of tailored business suits are over. Offices have given way to open seating, and the days of respect based strictly on position title are a thing of the past.

Recently, a candidate for a sales associate position at Investis Digital was introduced to me (Don) as she was making the rounds for her interview. In her first words to me, she asked if I had a couple of minutes to discuss our strategy with her. I agreed, which immediately took us into a discussion about the direction of our company, its mission, and the values we espoused.

To say the least, it was one of the more interesting interactions I have had in a very long time. The experience highlights the need for employees, even potential employees, to see the leader as who they really are. Meaning, does the wall of words match the person? Respect is earned in the 21st century through the ability to paint a vivid vision for anyone who asks, a vision that someone can tell you stand for and are committed to accomplishing ethically.

What Type of Leader Are You?

These types of changes in the workplace do not mean that all leaders should mimic one another and lead in the same cookie-cutter approach. In professional services, these are important distinctions. When understood through the lens of emotional intelligence, different types of leadership styles support particular cultural and organizational structures:

- **Transformational leadership instills a culture of inspiration.** Transformational leaders explore what defines the organization's culture and install changes to purposefully improve it. Here, leaders align the organization's goals and values with those of team members. Honest feedback is encouraged, which improves morale and productivity.

- **Service leadership develops a culture of inclusion.** The organizational pyramid is flipped onto its point, where everyone serves as a leader. The leader's task is to establish visionary goals and strategic direction with a focus toward the larger community. Meanwhile, the manager serves in a support role as employees work to achieve these objectives. Many successful professional services organizations embrace this type of "service-oriented" leadership.

- **Participative leadership creates a culture of innovation.** When relying on a democratic approach, leaders work to build consensus among team members through a process of compromise, collaboration, and consensus-building. Furthermore, the culture requires information sharing and an organizational structure that provides a voice to all team members.

- **Directive leadership reinforces a culture of consistency.** This is the most traditional—and most outdated—of the five types of leadership, where the organization is structured like a pyramid. Power flows from the top down, with specific instructions and tasks. Neither encourages collaborative culture nor dialogue and openness. In fact, within this type of structure, power is derived precisely from the opposite of dialogue and openness. It does, however, bring predictable results and consistent employee performance, but at the expense of agility, which ensures a scenario of "death by a thousand cuts" in the 21st century. In today's hypercompetitive environment, team members require flexibility to foster innovation and creativity. If a leader seeks an innovative organization but believes they can continue to use directive leadership, it is most certainly time for them to reevaluate their leadership style.

- **Authoritative leadership—perhaps the least appropriate type of leadership in our times—leads to a culture of compliance.** Authoritative leaders set the visionary direction of organizations and clearly explain the roles individual employees will play in determining that long-term vision. Leaders receive compliance out of fear, but then often struggle to foster an organizational culture of empowerment or professional development, without which innovation is stymied, if not wholly suffocated.

Traditional leadership, as seen in the last two leadership styles, does not inspire or connect with millennial or Gen Z workers. According to an article in *Forbes,*[4] millennial workers embrace a flat management structure that offers flexibility and a work–life balance. Flat structures also appeal to millennials because they seek a clear path for providing feedback as they push back against policy for policy's sake. When leadership does not meet millennial standards, they are more than willing to leave the company. Meanwhile, when millennials obtain leadership positions, they seek to empower and transform the teams they lead.

A conventional mistake is believing the role of a leader is to make the business successful. In reality, the role of a leader is to map out where the business needs to go, and why. The next step is to activate the vision by articulating it to employees; doing so creates a culture of commitment and ownership, which has the goal of empowering employees to make the business successful. When you bring teams together around a shared vision, anchored in your values, you create a culture of purpose and unity that builds momentum. Things in motion stay in motion; that's Physics 101, it's also Purpose 101. So when there is momentum, there are increased efficiencies. Ultimately, the result is an increase in profitability.

Leadership, Purpose, and the Service-Profit Chain

The concept of the service-profit chain—the set of activities undertaken by a firm to deliver profits—has been around for years. When you add purpose to the service-profit chain, you get happy employees, which lead to happy customers, which lead to greater profits. Again, your actions as a leader are meant to bring the values and purpose of the business to life so that all stakeholders, not just employees, participate." When the values are clear, work is completed with purpose. When purpose is driving the momentum, energy is directed at accomplishing tasks and projects more productively and more happily. This results in a drastic increase in employee retention, happier clients, less client churn, and increased profit margins.

Look to the Three Keys

In the last chapter, we explored how a leader defines and drives culture inside the company. Everyone in the organization rallies around the purpose, values, and story, infusing everything they do with a sense of shared culture, which collectively directs the business where it needs to go. To align everyone toward the vision, a leader must build a strong culture anchored by uncompromising values. In a business, as discussed in the introduction, values are twofold:

- Core values that define you as an individual and leader. Values on this level underpin and guide your decisions and behaviors.
- Shared values that define your organization. Values at this level serve to show the spectrum of internal and external stakeholders the scope and purpose of the organization. They also directly influence the culture and climate of the workplace.

Leaders are fulfilled and without conflict when they hold fast to both their own values and the organization's shared values. When a CEO leads with their organization's shared values, they lead with greater clarity and authenticity. Shared values offer a reliable guide and framework for orienting employees, goals, and each person's individual decisions within the company.

Internally, transparency surrounding company goals and values filters down from the CEO to those we lead. When employees are given these valuable tools, they find leaders easier to understand and predict. Employees have greater clarity around what we want and expect from them and can use this knowledge to guide how they work. Externally, transparency about goals and values floats up to your board of directors and clients. Simply put, stakeholders are more likely to experience the *why* of your decisions and leadership behaviors more than the *what* or *how*.

Behave Like a Leader

Purposeful, intentional leaders guide their people to be dynamic, excited, and inspired to make the everyday decisions necessary to drive the mission forward. Great leaders are self-aware. They consistently live and behave in line with their values. Most importantly, they understand, appreciate, and grow with and alongside their team members.

Self-awareness is a critical factor in identifying your core values; how can you know your values if you don't know who you are? And if you don't know who you are, it is nearly impossible for employees in a service firm to know who you are, either. Self-awareness is a linchpin for productive daily interactions with team members, clients, and stakeholders. When you are self-aware of how your behavior influences and impacts others, you act with empathy and authenticity. This becomes an example for your team and they respond in kind.

We cannot emphasize enough the importance of knowing your strengths, but, at the same time, don't believe your press clippings— know who you are and who you are not. There are hundreds, if not thousands, of psychometric tests to determine your strengths and weaknesses. (We talk about our favorite, CliftonStrengths, in the Appendix.) A trusted coach or mentor can also provide insight into behaviors you may not be able to see within yourself.

Be Consistent

Leadership and consistency go hand in hand. Leaders show every employee the way forward, whether times are good or bad. Leadership is synonymous with dependability, and consistent behavior leads to dependability. In professional services, this is a critical attribute in the 21st century.

Your employees, clients, and vendors all rely on you. When they can predict your behavior, you create a safe space where they know what will happen in particular situations or points of communication. This is crucial when unforeseen challenges arise. Fact: employees follow dependable leaders. When you're consistent, your teams learn, and eventually know, they can rely on you. People want to know that the person they work for is the same dependable person and leader all day, every day.

The Water Bottle

Fran uses a very practical example in discussing consistency to drive the point home:

"We were working on several challenging projects simultaneously, one of which was with a difficult, demanding client. Her project had a lot of moving parts, and when things happened that were beyond my control, I tended to react emotionally and inconsistently. I did not understand the importance of consistency until one defining moment with my project lead, Angelica.

Angelica always had a water bottle in her hand. She called me into a conference room and closed the door. She slammed the water bottle on the table and the lid fell off. Water sloshed everywhere and neither of us moved to wipe it up. She had my full attention.

She locked on my eyes and from a place of trust, love, and respect, said, "On a given day, I never know which Fran I am going to get. This [behavior] is a problem that needs to be resolved. Our client hired you for your guidance on how to solve their problem because they do not know how to do it."

Having the courage to call out your boss on their behavior is extremely difficult, but in an organization that values openness and lives a purpose-driven culture, leaders need to be both willing to accept the criticism and to take action.

I owned my behavior and said, "You deserve better, and they deserve better. I owe it to you to be completely present to empower you to make the decisions you need to make regardless of what might be going on around us that is out of our control."

Angelica was 100 percent right. I am grateful for this experience because it helped to remind me what is expected of a leader at all times, with no exception. Leaders never get a day off, period.

As a leader, your energy always impacts the room. Being attuned to the members of your team and acknowledging them and their concerns creates respect, which leads to more dynamic collaboration. Keeping your purpose clear becomes a self-guiding system throughout the organization and keeps everyone on track to achieve the mission.

Know and Grow Your Team

Chapter 4 explores hiring and developing your team, but from a leadership point of view, you have to get to know your team and make sure they are aware how important their continued growth is to you. To invest intelligently in your employee's growth requires you to know their interests and desires.

There are myriad specific communications tools you can leverage with your team—and clients—to learn specifics about them so you can develop integrated strategies for helping them grow. We like one tool in particular and have found it to be effective in empowering leaders to be open to constructive criticism, new ideas, and approaches. We call this the ABCDE rule. The rule:

- Creates an environment where team members are valued and are significantly more likely to contribute

- Allows leaders to get to facts and specifics that enable the team to reach resolutions quickly

Statements have to be made without these actions:

- Assume: you cannot assume something you don't know for a fact.
- Blame: you cannot blame other people for the situation.
- Complain: you cannot complain about what happened.
- Defend: you cannot defend what you've done.
- Excuse: you cannot make excuses, period.

The ABCDE rule proactively forces conversations to move forward productively by focusing on where the company is going and what the company is committed to doing, rather than emotionally rehashing what already happened and whose fault it was. The rule is exceptionally good at identifying red flags and roadblocks so team members can move through them fast and reach decisions quickly. The goal is to find the issue and fix it. An overly optimistic and nondirected enthusiastic exchange between employees can lead down a faulty path to poor decisions just as quickly as a heated finger-pointing argument can.

Each interaction—whether a daily email exchange, a meeting, or a team-building event—is an opportunity to learn something new about the team and provide insight into strategies for mentorship that will elevate them past those challenges.

What Can You Do?

A focus on balancing talent development with organizational goal achievement places a company on the trajectory toward success. However, motivating team members toward achieving those goals is no small task. Leaders must:

- Create a clear vivid vision.
- Understand and embody the organizational culture 24/7.

- Focus on employee personal and professional development.
- Reflect behaviors that inspire and motivate others to change.
- Encourage innovation through collaboration.

In the next chapter, we will explore how to hire and develop leaders across the organization.

Notes

1. http://boston.goarch.org/assets/files/your%20leadership%20is %20unique.pdf
2. John P. Kotter, *Leading Change* (Cambridge, MA: Harvard Business Review Press, 2012).
3. https://www.forbes.com/sites/lizryan/2016/03/27/management-vs-leadership-five-ways-they-are-different/#2419e17d69ee
4. https://www.forbes.com/sites/kimberlyfries/2018/01/18/7-ways-millennials-are-changing-traditional-leadership/#20ffb4a87dae

4

Hire Leaders

Hiring people is an art, not a science, and resumes can't tell you whether someone will fit into a company's culture.
—*Howard Schultz, former Chief Executive and Executive Chairman of Starbucks*

The leadership story of Ernest Shackleton has been told for decades. More than a hundred years after his expeditions, their relevance to business is clear. In fact, a Harvard Business School professor has even written a case study on the leadership lessons from Shackleton and his expeditions. Shackleton tried to reach the South Pole twice between 1901 and 1913. During each expedition, he made significant scientific discoveries, climbed Mount Erebus, and got closer to the South Pole than anyone else had up to that point, but he never reached his goal. In 1914, he decided to make a third expedition and, legend has it, advertised for crew by placing a newspaper ad (Figure 4.1):

Men wanted for hazardous journey. Low wages, bitter cold, long hours of complete darkness. Safe return doubtful. Honor and recognition in the event of success.

Shackleton is claimed to have received five thousand applicants! Can you imagine narrowing down five thousand applicants to the twenty-seven he required? He sorted them into piles: nut cases who wanted to do something strange, the hopeless with nothing else going on in their lives, those with potential, and so on. He interviewed many and selected the twenty-seven *lucky* fellows who accompanied him to the Antarctic in an attempt to reach the South Pole.

During that expedition, his boat got trapped in the ice. The crew abandoned the boat and lived on floating ice. Then they set off in three small boats, eventually reaching Elephant Island. Shackleton took five crew members and went for help. He returned and rescued all of them. Ten months later, the boat sank. Despite the ad that said essentially, "It may not turn out well for you," not one person died.

The ad—arguably one of the world's most legendary job postings—was remarkable for its strong, honest, and direct language.

Figure 4.1   Thousands of men responded to this newspaper ad.

Though his accomplishments went largely uncelebrated in the years after his death, Shackleton has become a revered leadership figure.

The Shackleton ad copy has also taken on a life of its own, as hiring managers and entrepreneurs point to it as an example of how to lure exceptional people to your organization. Not only does the story suggest how to write a job ad, it also bears witness to an honest leader committed to his people and his vision.

While hiring practices have changed since Shackleton's time, effective and efficient hiring of quality talent has always been critical to professional service organizations. Yet, with the rise of millennials and their increased focus on meaningful work, recruiting and hiring has taken on even greater importance. Hiring quality talent now requires bringing corporate values front and center in the process. In this chapter, you will learn exactly how purpose-driven hiring should be done and further explore the critical nature of culture alignment in professional services firms.

The Hiring Process Has Changed

Recruiting, developing, and retaining talent contributes to a professional service organization's productivity and growth. Without strong talent, an organization cannot survive and transform. Without transformation, an organization cannot grow. New innovations in recruiting can help you find high-quality candidates, but only if recruiters know how to adapt and use values as the ultimate barometer of fit. The rule of thumb in a purpose-driven firm is to hire for fit first, not for skills. You can always help the right employee learn a new set of skills. If you fail to follow this rule, you will only burn money hiring the wrong people until you change the way you recruit and hire.

Today, even with the increase in technology used in recruitment, the hiring process is actually far more personal than a few decades ago. Many jobs are found through referrals as well as online dialogues with other like-minded prospective hiring managers. Job boards have evolved from a list of links to sophisticated platforms that match job seekers with employers based on skill sets and mutual alignment. Empirical studies[1] have shown that a significant number of jobs today are found using social networks—and not just LinkedIn. Recruiters and employers use their social media presence to communicate their brand and values. Corporate websites highlight the numerous reasons why they are a great company to work for. Your firm's online presence, including its website and social media, must clearly demonstrate that you live your values and purpose every day. Be authentic and transparent in what you communicate online. Ultimately, by the time a candidate applies for a position, that person already has some idea about how he or she fits into the company culture.

For candidates and companies, the job search and recruitment process are two sides of the same coin. They both require connection and the building of relationships. For example, it is common for an executive to move from one company to another and then recruit former team members to the new organization. In that situation, not only is the person hired someone whose work is familiar to you, but you also know that they align with your values. That's why they were hired! Effective recruiters use related tactics, though they likely didn't work with the candidate. They look for culture fit, technical skills, and openness, and more and more rely on data and analytics to predict potential employee success.

In the not too distant past, star applicants competed for jobs by showing off their talents in a competition that rivaled a beauty pageant. Today, employers are the contestants that must compete to attract and hire the best talent. Firms promote aspects of their culture and values that appeal to the candidates from new generations of job seekers. For example, career flexibility, such as the possibility of working remotely, holds a high priority in the ranks of modern job seekers. Savvy employers highlight their communications systems, which allow for collaboration anywhere via a choice of channels. Leading firms also demonstrate the importance and availability of opportunities to learn and grow on the job, which is another desire of today's younger professional cohort.

Everyone Wants to Work at Advantages

While it's true that employers compete to draw the best talent, companies known to offer a great culture often have more applicants than they can process. Fran's company, Advantages, made the *Inc.* 50 Best Places to Work list and in the months following, not a week went by that she didn't receive multiple requests for employment and even offers from people willing to work for free. That sounds like an employer's dream, as Fran notes, "Even someone who works for free has to be trained—and that's a cost to the team."

The actual interview has changed, too. Improvements in technology allow for online interview scheduling and videoconference interviews. Applicants have multiple touchpoints with your organization before the first interview even takes place. More than ever, candidates push for a shorter, tighter interview process and fewer hoops to jump through.

And while you are interviewing candidates, remember they are also interviewing you. Today's job seekers want to know what you stand for and how your organization contributes to the greater good in the world. Organizations cognizant of these shifts cultivate values that meet the changing demands of the job market and have an advantage when looking to hire talent. If your firm does not want to lose good candidates to its competition, it needs to embrace values and learn to lead a culture that shares them.

Align Values and People

Leading professional services organizations with cultures that reflect their values will want to hire only people who share those values. Research shows that when a team of employees share the same values, a very powerful force is created. According to Gallup[2] research from 2017, a 10 percent increase in employee connection to a firm's values or purpose prompted an 8.1 percent decrease in turnover and a 4.4 percent increase in profitability. Imagine the business results possible if your team was 50 percent better connected or, ideally, 100 percent connected to the firm's values and purpose. It is for this reason that leading firms and star employees alike focus on cultural fit over specific qualifications and salary. The right employees for your organization must be driven by your organization's mission.

Some people prefer doing repetitive tasks. These employees love efficiency and feel validated by delivering high-quality work in their targeted tasks. However, if they are suddenly required to think on their feet and manage tasks differently, they may experience frustration because now the job requirements don't match their preferred working style. Other people thrive in more ambiguous work environments. These employees love facing different challenges every day and always want to work on the biggest, riskiest accounts.

It is likely that your business requires both employees who like repetitive tasks and those who are curious thrill-seekers. More important, however, is that personal values and beliefs of the people you hire align with the company's shared values. If a core value of your firm is respecting a set schedule (i.e. you expect people to show up for work at a certain time), and a candidate under consideration values flexible hours, the two of you may not be a good match.

Hire the Best Available Athlete

Consistent with hiring for fit and training for skill, one practice that has served Don well over the years is to hire the best available athlete.

The concept of "best available athlete" has been popularized by the NFL Draft, whereby a team may opt to select a player during the draft based not on a particular position, but rather on which available athlete is the fastest, most nimble, strongest, and so on. After drafting, the team will insert the player into a position, in which he naturally fits and is most needed. The ultimate goal is to make the team better by building around the best possible players.

In the same vein, when a job candidate walks into the office, you may realize that you're not sure where they belong in the current organization. But they come in with a positive attitude and are willing to do whatever it takes to be successful. They leave their ego at the door and you immediately recognize this person as a keeper. They don't have the specific skill set you may be looking for, but you have the sense that hiring this person would add substantially to the organization.

My experience has shown me that this is a winning strategy. It is what I call hiring the best available athlete. I look for someone who fits our culture, shares our values, and brings strong leadership skills. My experience has shown me that this is a winning strategy. These are the type of people upon whom we can build a successful company, and I wish I could find more like them.

What does a successful hire look like? In a purpose-driven firm, it is a candidate who aligns with your values, aligns with your culture, and is interested in staying for a long time. Successful hiring comes from the nuance of drawing alignment between personal core values of the prospect and the firm's shared values. "Hire for fit first, train for skill" is rule number one. If you shift the hiring mindset and embrace this fundamental rule, your firm will end up hiring employees who enjoy coming to work every day, and from their first day on the job feel like they've always been a part of your team.

Invest in Your Hiring Process

Being great at recruiting doesn't just happen. Excellent recruiting requires a structured process, an actionable plan, and companywide buy-in. If executed properly, the firm will reduce its risk for bad hires and increase its chances of hiring top performers.

Myriad technology tools exist to support an effective process for the recruiting and hiring of candidates. Particularly useful, applicant-tracking software equips your team with interview plans, scheduling and reviewing for each role you are trying to fill. Software like this makes it easier to evaluate multiple candidates and ensure you gather the information you need to make the right hiring decision.

The Shortlist

Fran writes specific ads to attract candidates who will align with Advantage's values.

When I'm looking for new employees, I speak like Shackleton did, I tell them the truth. I am not easy to work for and I have high expectations, but I'm good as gold. I'm passionate about our vision and dream. So when looking for employees, I start with our core values and always aim to hire for fit.

Some years ago, I placed a help-wanted ad for an assistant. Within three or four days I received seventy applications, but had no time to review all of them. Around the same time, I went to a networking event and brought up this difficulty. My peers thought I was crazy. They would kill for seventy applicants. I thought *they* were crazy; I wanted as few qualified responses as possible to my ads. I wanted my ad to filter out bad fits and attract a select handful of applicants who would be a good culture fit.

We developed a simple, but not easy, process that acts to deter candidates who are unlikely to fit our culture. We post ads that paint a picture of the core values that are important to us, along with the skill set or abilities that go with the job. If the ad grabs a candidate's attention, we ask them to send us a video answering three questions, one of which requests their personal "why." If they don't respond with the video, they are automatically eliminated. If they do, the candidates are sent another five questions to answer. These include: why are you a good fit for the role, and what do you bring to the role. More than 50 percent of the original applicants never respond. They self-select out. The people who follow through immediately demonstrate why they'd be a good fit to work in our environment.

If an ad gets fewer than twelve replies, that's success for me. However, it's not about the numbers. This process has done wonders for my business outcomes. I've been following this process in my hiring for about seven years. In that time, I have never had to fire someone. Further, team members want to stay with Advantages even if they have to transition to remote worker or contractor status. Our employee retention does amazing things that impact our success. Just one example is our annual strategic planning, which is greatly accelerated because the level of trust between long-term employees is extremely high—we can cut through a lot of BS and get right to work.

Involve the CEO

Employees who choose to work for your firm are buying into you, the leader, and your vision, which is all the more reason the CEO should be involved in hiring. Google co-founder and Alphabet CEO, Larry Page, personally reviews each new candidate the company hires.[3] (In 2015 Google hired about six thousand people.) He says, "It helps me to know what's really going on." If Larry Page can't convince you to participate in the hiring process, maybe these three reasons from other CEOs can:

1. Ensure culture fit.

Solutions to problems and performance require leadership. To lead, is to recruit and build culture. One of the biggest hiring mistakes is spending too much interview focus on technical chops rather than on culture fit. Culture fit makes up 60 percent of the reason why new hires succeed or fail.

—*Dave Carvajal, CEO at Davepartners.com*

2. More time spent hiring equals less time spent fixing mistakes.

At most companies, people spend 2 percent of their time recruiting and 75 percent managing their recruiting mistakes.

—*Richard Fairbank, CEO at Capital One*

3. Know the true cost of hiring.

Early on, I understood the ultimate cost of hiring, not only in dollars but also in time and energy and the value to my company. No one wants to needlessly throw away money and certainly no one has an abundance of time they can afford to waste. If I don't get this part right, nothing following will matter.

—*Aytekin Tank, founder and CEO of online form builder JotForm*

When hiring for cultural fit, both the company and the potential new hire need to be honest and vulnerable. If a leader can expose their own vulnerability and provide a safe place for the new hire to do the same, an emotional connection happens. From there you earn their trust and they can then let their skills shine.

Interviewing with the Three Keys

It is important to get granular for a moment and better understand what can be done in the actual interview process to maximize results. First off, the walls between the interviewer and candidate need to come down. It is a two-way street and both the candidate and interviewer should be relaxed and eager to engage.

When you're interviewing, keep your Three Keys in mind—purpose, values, and story. Does the candidate's moral and ethical character match that of your organization? What is the candidate's personal "why" and how has that impacted them in unexpected situations? Are they loyal and committed to the mission of your firm? The answers to such questions are the key to purposeful hiring. Surprisingly, candidates often give different answers in different environments. So, speak with each candidate in multiple locations; for example, hold one interview in the office and another in a coffee shop.

As providers of advice and guidance and developers of intellectual property, professional services firms need to go beyond what resumes say and get to know how candidates think. Even when top consulting firms interview candidates graduating from business school, they rarely ask about their college experience. Interviewers present a verbal case study and ask candidates how they would handle the situation. Provide your candidates the opportunity to understand and experience your mission during the interview.

If a candidate's work history has gaps or numerous jobs, remember that the markets fluctuate. Employees get let go because of downsizing and sometimes even good employees simply get fired. Honesty, a core value most firms respect, remains the best policy. A candidate who says, "I got laid off, and in retrospect, I could have done things differently. Maybe it wouldn't have made a difference because the company was in bad shape, but it's something I've considered," is showing personal responsibility, emotional intelligence, and self-awareness—all qualities that can make for an excellent employee.

During the interview process, look for inspiration and passion. Is the candidate enthusiastic about what they are doing or do they seem to be going through the motions? Have candidates tell you their story, in their own words, and ask for details. Their passion will shine through when you tap into stories that highlight their core values.

With these details you can evaluate more clearly how an individual might fit with the firm's shared values.

Is it clear that the candidate is evaluating their own fit with your culture? How are their listening skills? You've probably heard the adage, "We have two ears and one mouth so we can listen twice as much as we speak." The conversation should be a two-way affair with questions from the candidate that highlight their values, career goals, and expectations from the firm. If you are the only one asking questions, that's not a good sign.

Candidates should demonstrate an understanding of your mission. Have they researched the company? Do they ask informed questions? Are they curious about the future of the business and how they can help further its success? The list of questions that can be asked is limitless. The objective is to ask questions that elicit the candidate's values and help you determine if this person fits with the firm's culture.

Interview for Leadership Qualities

The Three Keys will guide you to look for candidates with leadership attributes that align with your purpose, values, and story. Ask yourself: What does a values-based purpose-driven leader look like in your organization? Where do values show up in your leaders? During the interview process, draw out the personal strengths and values of potential leadership hires to see if they align with company culture. This is more important than scrutinizing their resume.

RecruitLoop[4] offers eight job candidate qualities that demonstrate leadership potential:

- They show a higher level of engagement.
- They're comfortable with failure.
- They have great communication skills.
- They know when to listen.
- They don't need to show off.
- They get the best out of others.
- They can multitask.
- They know that education never stops.

Hire Former Employees, But Not All of Them

In his own "Shackleton moments," Don has been hired by several companies to repair a difficult situation. He says:

I look for opportunities where things are operationally suboptimal, but the solutions seem to be in my control. My thinking is that if I can fix it, there's great value to be generated and gained.

When I first take on a role, I find someone who's worked with me before and—much like Shackleton's ad—I say, "Hey, do you want to join me at this operational mess? The equity may not be worth anything, the pay's probably bad, but we'd be in this together. Let's go turn it into something." The good ones always say yes.

For some period, I slog through the mess, wondering why I took the job in the first place. Then things start improving, I begin to see value, and then in true entrepreneurial, hockey-stick fashion, things take off. The market begins to notice, and the company is thought of as an up-and-comer—like the actor who's been working for twenty years and becomes an "overnight success" when a film hits it big. Nobody writes about the slog, but the press loves an "overnight success."

When the word is out about the company's success, then people from my past come out of the woodwork. I'll get an email that reads, "Hi, Don, I used to work for you back in the day. Remember me? I'd love to work for you again. I hear great things are happening." These aren't the people I need, or look for, and neither should you. Find the people who are willing to get in the quagmire with you from day one. They are the most valuable. They understand your vision, the path you are trying to create, and what's involved in getting you there.

Afterward, when it is all over, there's a certain character in these same people who stay in contact for a long period of time. They can't wait to sign up and do it all again.

Link Hiring to Your Bottom Line

Invest in a structured hiring process to ensure the acquisition of the best-aligned talent. Then continue to invest in that talent. When employees feel valued, they are more loyal. Loyal employees are great employees. Investing in hiring the right people maximizes returns for your organization. The quality of hire has direct ties to your company's financial performance in two fundamental ways:

- The significant cost associated with hiring the wrong people
- The positive performance impact from improved productivity, better teamwork, and greater efficiencies from hiring the right people

The Cost of a Bad Hire

Dr. Brad Smart, founder of the Topgrading hiring methods, has determined that the average cost of a bad hire can be roughly fifteen times an employee's base salary. Additionally, the Center for Economic and Policy Research offers an online calculator[5] to help management estimate the cost of employee turnover at their firm. The math speaks for itself; bad decisions in new hires are expensive.

Some costs are clear. If you hired a headhunter, you know how much money you spent acquiring headhunted talent. If you have an in-house talent acquisition team, you should know how much money you spent on job advertisements. These are all specific sunk costs. However, this data does not provide a full picture of what bad hires truly costs. Add up the time each of your employees spent recruiting, interviewing, and training this employee. What impact did he or she have on company financial performance? Did the bad hire impact your culture in ways that affected the rest of your teams? These costs associated with these issues will dwarf what you spent in headhunter fees and ads that result in the wrong people.

Tony Hsieh, CEO of Zappos, admitted in an interview[6] that hiring is the biggest category of mistakes at the company. "If you add up the costs of all the bad decisions the bad hires make . . . and on top of those, the bad hires that made other bad hires, over the course of Zappos' history, it's probably cost us well over 100 million dollars." He even discourages his new hires after the first day, offering anyone $2,000 not to return the next day to further weed out those who don't fit. Now, that is a full-on commitment to hiring for fit.

Hire Slow, Fire Fast

Even after spending significant time and effort to find someone for a particular role, the new hire may not work out. Because our work in professional services can be fluid, it can be difficult to give up on a new hire. It can be tempting to think, in time they will "come around." That almost never happens.

It's no surprise that the best way to avoid bad hires is to get better at hiring. Tony Hsieh reduced his losses at Zappos by changing the company's hiring principles; instead of hiring as fast as possible to fill roles quickly, Zappos hires slowly. Taking the time to implement a process has helped Zappos identify top performers who are the right fit for their organization.

But understand, even after taking all the precautions, gathering all the right information, and asking the revealing questions, you still may make the wrong hiring decisions. When a bad hire happens, appreciate how difficult the hiring process can be, but do not wait to correct the error. The opportunity and financial cost in waiting is significant.

When Bad Hires Happen

Fran has a pretty strong record of making good hires, but during the writing of this book, one hire turned out to be a mis-hire. She says:

My team—per my instructions and our values—hired for fit, but in this case, didn't test for skill. My team did everything right culturally, but they didn't ask enough questions to learn about the candidate's ability to think strategically and manage people.

The person we hired was a perfect fit for our culture—not overly polished, a single millennial (meaning he has time to work), and he was looking to build a career. We learned within his first two weeks, however, that he didn't have the skills for the job, which meant training him for a job he's paid well to already know how to do. I showed him what needed to be done and outlined my expectations, but he couldn't pick up the ball and run with it. Within a week, it was clear he wasn't a good fit. We mutually, and quickly, agreed that he would move on.

Invest in and Grow Your People

Mike Krzyzewski, Duke University basketball coach, said, "Each group and each youngster is different. As a leader or coach, you get to know what they need." Developing purposeful leaders often means noticing potential in others and lighting the spark within them to do more or become more.

The Butterfly

One young woman, Christel, came to work at Fran's firm, Advantages, as a junior designer. She grew up in the firm, and was given the nickname, the Butterfly. Christel would step into a role, absorb everything there was to know about that role, become a success in that role, and then move on to another one. She was always interested in taking on more responsibility. In seven years, Christel changed positions five or six times. Over time, she worked her way up from a junior-level employee to become a respected leader at the firm.

When you have an employee with that type of curiosity and drive, recognize it so that you can guide them to cultivate their own growth. She asked proactive questions and demonstrated a desire for personal and professional growth. However, she also took advantage of the tools our firm has in place to help her achieve her metamorphosis. Our performance scorecard process provides a collaborative platform for employees to bring personal passion to their work that benefits the company. For Christel, this meant professional growth and exploring new roles. For others, it might involve something more personal such as sharing an outside interest that leads to new perspectives. Every year, goals and expectations are drafted and aligned to ensure professional development of the entire team on an individualized basis. This is part of our shared values, and Christel was the embodiment of them through her career.

To invest in your employees' growth, you have to know their interests and desires. When you bring on new hires, spend sufficient time getting to know them. A specific recommendation could be to allot fifteen minutes a day to such acclimation. Encourage them to ask whatever they want, provide support, guide them, and satisfy their curiosity. Over time, reduce the meetings to two or three times per week, and eventually taper off to a much lower frequency. These conversations help you spot diamonds in the rough.

Do not just focus on what the company is going to get from your employees. Invest in all aspects of your employees—not just their work growth, but also their personal growth. In a values-based organization, it is no longer enough to think of a project manager as simply a role; you need to think of the individual, who sits in that project manager role.

When you make investments to support employee growth, that investment will ultimately yield substantial benefits for the company. The more your leaders grow, the more the company grows. You can't be on top of everyone. The only way to make sure you're delivering a quality service is to have good people working on those projects. When you invest in your people and let them know their work is valued, you keep them engaged. If you take care of them, they'll take care of the clients, and ultimately you.

Sometimes your good employees will leave the organization, but they will remember what they learned and how they were treated by the leaders in the firm. Other employees will change roles and grow within the organization. Your firm benefits from having a succession plan that facilitates these transitions and encourages in-house employee growth.

Plan for Leadership Succession

When thinking about scaling your organization and planning for the future, you can't help but think about leadership succession. Who will fill the void of leaders who are promoted or leave the firm? Who might succeed you? Purpose-driven leaders think about succession planning from their first day on the job.

Succession plans are used to address the inevitable changes that occur when employees resign, retire, are fired, get sick, or die. They make sure the business is prepared for all contingencies by identifying and training high-potential workers for advancement into key roles.

Succession planning is often considered only at the most senior levels in an organization. But the reality is that everyone on your team, from the lowest-level new hire to the most tenured executive, should be thinking about advancing and replacing themselves. Engaging everyone in their own succession planning is a strategy for identifying and developing future leaders at your company at all levels.

Succession is a business process that must happen to keep your firm running smoothly. It is a manageable event, not a major organizational crisis. When your in-house superstars are battle-tested and culturally aligned, you will not only have significant retention advantages; you will have a pool of waiting leaders.

Proactive Succession Planning

Your organization's Three Keys should be reflected in any leadership succession plan. Keeping potential leaders at the managerial level in conversations about succession and sharing your succession planning with human resources and your board of directors will help ensure that the plan maintains alignment with firm values.

It takes time to identify and prepare a promising candidate to take over a leadership role. Every leader should focus on developing team members for future positions. Start the day that someone new joins the firm, even if you don't think you'll need a replacement in the near future. When you prep a strong employee to assume an important role, you create an invaluable safety net. Ultimately, succession starts from aligned values during the hiring process. Are you bringing potential future leaders who share your values into the firm?

When the time comes to fill a role, the obvious successor may be the second in command, but don't disregard other promising employees. Look for people who best display the raw talent and characteristics necessary to thrive in higher positions, regardless of their current title. This aligns with the "best athlete available" hiring theory espoused by Don earlier in the chapter. Plan to put your "best athletes" in leadership roles, and they will make your succession plans easier. If there are questions about the suitability of an internal leader, a vacation is a great time to have a potential successor step in to assume some responsibilities. The employee will gain experience while you learn how prepared the person is to take on a bigger role.

Succession Planning Influences Hiring

Once internal candidates are identified as potential successors for various key roles in your organization, take note of any talent gaps. In this way, it is possible to use the succession planning process to help identify where to focus your recruiting efforts.

In an instructive article, "The holy grail of effective leadership succession planning: How to overcome the succession planning paradox,"[8] Deloitte highlights a number of worthwhile considerations, condensed here:

1. Make succession planning worthwhile for the people most affected by its results. Asking leaders to fully engage in succession planning without an emphasis on their own interests is likely to result in apathy and avoidance. An organization that does succession planning well will align incentives and development opportunities for both the incumbent and the successor.

   Incumbent leaders need to be motivated to take an active role in developing successors. It is often wrongly assumed that talent will be ready for the next role without much involvement from current leaders.

2. Establish accountability and advocacy. Having one or more senior-level advocates for succession planning is crucial in building an effective succession culture in the organization. Succession planning should be championed as a critical growth lever by these senior leaders, or it risks being considered a "nice to have" and not being discussed on the executive agenda.

   Additionally, organizations with effective succession management practices push accountability for succession planning down through all levels of the business.

3. Orient toward the future. At its core, succession planning is about preparing your firm for the future. Yet ironically, many organizations build their succession processes around the needs of current roles, not what those roles will look like in the future.

   Orienting succession processes toward the future rather than the present needs yields two key benefits. The first is that it helps prepare the next generation of leaders to deal with a world that will differ, possibly drastically, from the present.

   Second, focusing on future decision-making related to future roles can help address concerns of "being put out to pasture," making the discussions less threatening for current leaders focused on self-preservation.

4. Create short-term goals to sustain a long-term focus. Succession planning is a long-term discipline in a short-term world. Leaders are often too busy with day-to-day firefighting to spare thought

and time for longer-term decisions; hence, succession planning remains low on their list of priorities. Organizations can break the task down into smaller, shorter-term components.

Establish tools, processes, and messaging to cultivate transparency and trust. Many employees, and even organizational leaders, often feel that leadership succession and planning is done within a "black box," without the transparency and simplicity necessary to inspire trust in the process. Organizations that use simple, accessible, and transparent data collection processes for succession planning and clearly communicate succession decisions using this data are more successful.

Investment as an Opportunity to Grow

One of the more important lessons to learn when creating a purpose-driven culture based on values is thinking about investment in your people as much more than access to seminars or education. Investment should be made in seeing how each individual employee responds to calls for leadership. Invest in determining the leadership potential of individuals. Expose potential leaders to new and challenging internal and external experiences. For example, an employee with leadership potential could shadow the project lead for a client and then fill in as a lead on a small or limited-scope project. Internally, have potential leaders conduct a town hall meeting or take charge of a philanthropic endeavor. Set expectations, teach by example, and encourage people to continually expand their capabilities and skills as part of growing with your firm.

Compensation

Regardless of the business, compensation is nearly always a challenging component of management. When trying to run a professional services firm that is driven by the Three Keys, there are added considerations, particularly with regard to today's younger professionals.

Money-focused compensation plans work well for those individuals who are motivated by money, but as we have seen, not everyone is motivated by money. In fact, today's employees are motivated by a sense of personal fulfillment, engagement, and growth. They are even willing to earn less to work with like-minded people and companies with whom their values align. Therefore, the compensation system you design for your firm should directly reflect its purpose and values.

The reality is that compensation at the senior or partner level and the non-partner tiers will have significant variation. The ultimate incentive for the most ambitious members of a professional services firm will remain the achievement of partner status, in whatever form that presents itself at your company. We'll briefly address general concepts for compensation at both levels. Let's start at the non-partner level.

Non-partner Incentive and Compensation

There are as many options for compensation as there are currencies in the world. There are, however, some basic concepts that are helpful when creating a plan. *Forbes* author Ian Altman, in his article "Compensation Plans that Drive Results,"[9] suggests four areas for improving your compensation plan:

- Build Accountability
- Split the Pie
- Handle Discounting
- Reward Consistency

To summarize Altman's concepts, "Build Accountability" means ensuring that the firm's financial incentives are linked to a combination of individual, team, and company performance. The majority should be focused on individual performance. In addition to the standard financial metrics, include metrics for how employees live and infuse their tasks and responsibilities with your purpose and culture. (This idea is discussed further in Chapter 9.) Everyone in the firm needs to be incentivized to take accountability for the success of the firm, at whatever level they operate, from the receptionist to the CEO.

In order to "Split the Pie," we must recognize that the sales process in professional services firms is not as straightforward as the process in a product-based company. There are several steps, from identifying an opportunity—which may come from a consultant or advisor who is not part of the business development team—to the scoping and development of the project, to the signing of the contract, followed by the actual work and results. Splitting the pie incentivizes employees to be part of the whole process and speaks to the inclusive feeling many employees seek. Clearly define the criteria to earn credit. This could ultimately become part of a larger compensation and review process where demonstration of revenue generation is rewarded.

In terms of "Handle Discounting," the key idea is to ensure that those involved in the sales process are disincentivized from price reductions that result in lower-margin business. Revenue recognition should be tied to discounting, or hopefully, the lack thereof. As professional services firms are often working on bespoke projects with flexible fee schedules, this may be less of an issue for some firms, but quite critical in others.

Finally, "Reward Consistency" is the surest way to keep your revenue on target. When your sales, business development, and even client service teams consistently meet their various targets, reward their efforts. Consistent performance helps firms deliver on their promises to their clients and employees. Remember, alignment on the firm's purpose, values, and story supports and leads to consistent behaviors and performance.

Alternative Methods of Compensation

Cash compensation is what provides the ability for your workers to continue showing up and doing their jobs. However, as noted, not everyone is strictly motivated by cash, and you may not have the cash, or may wish to use it for something other than remuneration.

Millennials and younger professionals are certainly more amenable to noncash forms of rewards and incentives, though many of these will also have a certain economic value to both the company and the employee.

The incentive of flexibility is certainly a compensation method worth exploring. If an option exists for remote work or alternative hours, that may work better for the employee. These are forms of compensation that many employees are willing to pursue.

Giving employees more time off, whether as vacation, sick days, or personal days, is a great way to compensate employees without offering greater cash compensation. Although there is a financial cost, as you must pay absent employees for their time off, the benefit often outweighs the costs in terms of employee satisfaction and productivity. Many technology-based professional services firms are adopting unlimited time-off policies as a part of the compensation programs. A longer-term incentive system in this vein is the sabbatical, where long-term employees receive extended periods off to explore different interests, which could be travel, personal, or philanthropic, and not necessarily related to the business or its goals.

Gone are the days of simple, standardized compensation packages based on position and years with the company. Compensation is part of the negotiation between employee and employer, and many routes can be taken to create effective incentives that satisfy employees while helping you reach your goals. In the end, alternative compensation can provide similar incentives as cash: improved productivity, better results for your clients, and happier employees.

Partner Compensation

At the most senior level—partner or executive—compensation takes on some very different elements.

Today, as with non-partner employees, there is no magic formula for partner compensation. One-size-fits-all rigid plans are unlikely to satisfy all your partners while meeting all your strategic goals. It will be an ongoing and evolving process as your firm and its needs change. The focus should be on ensuring the system set up is directly related to your strategic goals.

If you have actively gone through the process of defining your firm's values and purpose, creating a plan that aligns with these them will be easier. The plan must be transparent, clear, fair, and as simple as possible.

Compensate with Purpose

The important thing to remember in any compensation scheme that you develop for employees and partners is that your Three Keys should remain at the core and drive the decisions that you make. If a possible compensation practice doesn't meet your values or help drive your purpose, pick another one. There are plenty of ways to make it work.

Leadership, Purpose, and Performance

In professional services, the link between leadership and performance is relatively straightforward. The ability to influence the leadership skills of your team members to meet organizational demands is a complex element of the overall leadership development picture. Leaders are tasked with effectively guiding organizational goal achievement while considering the skills necessary for team members to produce the desired output.

Purposeful leaders beget purposeful leaders. A successful leader is defined by their succession—you may have heard the phrase "standing on the shoulders of giants." Each new leader emerges from the learning and groundwork of the leaders who came before them. It is a process of passing useful insights from generation to generation.

Existing leaders must nurture up-and-coming leaders. They must demonstrate what successful values-based leadership looks like and share their knowledge and experience. They should offer opportunities that expose leaders with different business perspectives to one another and foster a culture of purposeful risk-taking.

What Can You Do?

We can't say it enough: use the Three Keys to drive all the processes within your organization, including hiring and succession. When you clearly communicate your purpose, values, and story to people who are interested in working with you—through marketing, job ads, interview processes, and questions—the best matches come forward. People who don't align with your purpose and values are more likely to self-select out. To that end, consider the following when you're adding people to your firm:

- Incorporate your values into your company profile on LinkedIn and any job postings you release.
- Communicate your purpose and story when interviewing. You can see a person's skills on their resume; have a conversation that shows whether they're a good fit for your firm.
- Maintain ties with qualified employees from your previous engagements. People you know and respect should be among the first you approach when a new position opens.
- Shape future leaders by offering training and growth opportunity. There may not be an immediate clear path of succession, but by nurturing future leaders within your organization you will always have an internal pool from which to promote.

Now that you've filled your positions with qualified, motivated employees with leadership potential, Chapter 5 takes a look at how to structure your organization.

Notes

1. https://business.linkedin.com/content/dam/business/talent-solutions/global/en_us/c/pdfs/Ultimate-List-of-Hiring-Stats-v02.04.pdf
2. https://www.gallup.com/workplace/236279/three-ways-mission-driven-workplaces-perform-better.aspx
3. https://talkingtalent.prosky.co/articles/3-reason-why-ceos-should-be-involved-with-hiring
4. https://recruitloop.com/blog/8-ways-spot-leadership-potential-employees/
5. http://cepr.net/calculators/turnover_calc.html
6. https://www.inc.com/allison-fass/tony-hsieh-hiring-mistakes-cost-zappos-100-million.html
7. http://guides.wsj.com/management/recruiting-hiring-and-firing/how-to-reduce-employee-turnover/
8. https://www2.deloitte.com/content/dam/insights/us/articles/4772_Leadership-succession/DI_Succession-planning.pdf
9. https://www.forbes.com/sites/ianaltman/2016/11/17/compensation-plans-that-drive-results/#35aa97c8331a

5

The Purposefully
Structured Business

*Every company has two organizational structures: The
formal one is written on the charts; the other is the everyday
relationship of the men and women in the organization.*
—Harold Geneen, president and CEO, ITT, 1958–1977

Most business leaders understand that the corporate organizational
structure enables the efficient and productive functioning of a company. However, most professional services firms fail to give the design of
their organization sufficient focus. The evolution of departments, internal hierarchies, groups, and divisions within the company should be
explicit, particularly if your intent is to manage your firm with purpose.

The ideal structure of your organization should reflect and support your values and purpose, even though the size and specifics of
your business will change over time. For example, if your company
values innovation but organizes in a way that emphasizes repetitive
work, the firm will be challenged to take on projects that require

innovation. If you want to win innovative projects, the organization structure of the company must support innovation. Similarly, if open communication is a value, but your structure creates barriers to communication, the firm is not purposefully organized. When designing an organizational structure, one size does not fit all.

Regardless of the values the firm holds dear, the organization structure should be designed to ensure consistent communication of those values both inside and outside of the organization.

Sadly, many leaders think that organizational design has no relationship to the Three Keys of purpose, values, and story. In this chapter, you will explore how to purposefully create an organizational structure within the Three Keys paradigm.

Design Your Organization

The organizational structure may change over time as the company grows. A small company typically does not have the resources to create dedicated client or project teams. The risk inherent with dedicated teams lies in the division of work. The healthcare team may have an overload of business and struggle to get their work done while the consumer goods team sits idle. Small organizations need to be nimble and fluid to respond to workloads as they ebb and flow. As the firm grows, a client may request a dedicated team that works only on their account. For some companies such a request makes sense and they will reorganize to meet the client's need. Other companies may see the request as too disruptive. The decision to change your organization's structure depends on a number of factors.

As the company grows and matures, the organization structure tends to evolve organically to a point where it—usually—ends up with a more complex staff or functional organization.

Keep in mind that even when your organizational structure changes, the firm values remain the same. Regardless of the size or style of the structure, your values and beliefs yield a common purpose, which creates an emotional connection to everyone in the organization. This values-based connection your employees have with the firm allows you the flexibility to change your organization structure while still maintaining and growing with your current clients. Employees connect with these values and remain committed to the firm's overall mission and vision rather than a specific department or unit.

The remainder of this chapter focuses on the critical aspects of organizational structure and what it means to corporate performance in professional service organizations. We begin by examining the principal types of organizational structures:

- Line organizational structure
- Staff or functional authority organizational structure
- Line and staff organizational structure
- Divisional organizational structure
- Project organizational structure
- Matrix organizational structure

Line Organizational Structure

In a line organization (Figure 5.1), authority follows the chain of command and groups are divided by function. For example, finance people are grouped together and human resources people are grouped together. These functions service multiple internal and external clients, each function working separately toward the goals of the organization.

A line organization is easy to understand and simplifies the relationship between different levels present in the organization. The tasks and work at hand maintain flexibility, and decisions can be made quickly. Managers must have an in-depth knowledge about everything related to the business because employees are dependent on them for direction. This reliance on manager-specific knowledge means that as the organization grows, the structure becomes unproductive. Decisions tend to be funneled up through seniority and bottlenecks occur.

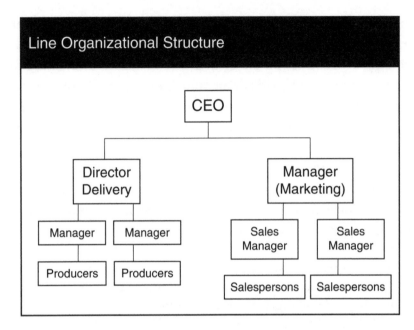

Figure 5.1   Line organizational structure.

A line organizational structure fits well for small professional service companies with values that emphasize efficiency and speed, but may not be aligned with a professional services company that values creativity, exploration, and out-of-the-box thinking.

Staff (or Functional) Organizational Structure

In a staff organizational structure (Figure 5.2), groups are divided by role or skill set—for example, a creative group, a project management group, or a client service group. The team members who do similar things work together in a dedicated group.

Staff or functional authority structures have the most knowledgeable managers and supervisors at the helm of each department to help the organization achieve its goals and grow. These leaders have direct authoritative power and make decisions quickly. However,

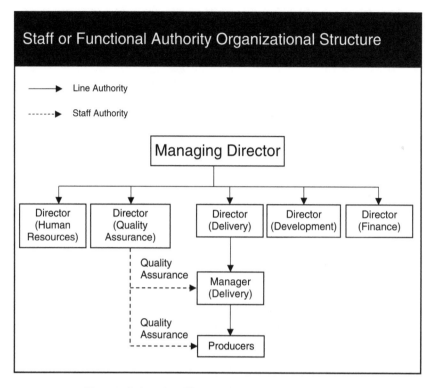

Figure 5.2   Staff organizational structure.

conflict arises when departmental or group level decisions end up impacting another group.

A staff organizational structure may be appropriate for a rapidly growing firm. With a diverse management group at the top of a hierarchical structure, the business can draw on broader expertise while retaining the central control that may be required by a firm's overall mission. The mission, once clearly and precisely defined, must be communicated to the leaders of each group. These individuals are responsible for the execution of the mission and making sure that employees follow their instructions to reach clearly defined goals. A staff organizational structure works well for professional services firms that emphasize growth and rapid accumulation of clients.

Staff Structures in a Small Firm

Fran finds a tremendous benefit to having leaders with multiple disciplines and experiences and being able to apply them to different sectors. She says:

We view our firm as walking a "three-legged race" with our clients. At Advantages, we have different divisions (a strategic division, a production and output division, a design division, etc.), but they're all built into the client experience. The client will always be connected to one of these divisions along with a client service leader, which may often be me, or a senior strategic leader. This creates the three legs—functional division and client service leadership, with the client in the middle. Depending on the client's project and needs, we can pull the team members with the most appropriate experience.

We don't specialize in a specific vertical, but rather align our efforts at a higher level with firm and client values. We seek an understanding of the client's strategy first and then align resources, budgets, and so on. We focus on getting unity and clarity within the internal team. It is this clarity that helps me manage our structure on a client-by-client basis, not based on vertical expertise.

When a potential client asks, "How many other companies within our vertical have you worked for?" I focus my response on our values of diversification and our fresh, nimble approach. In my experience, even if we have not been engaged previously in the specific vertical, we'll be awarded the project because clients see the value of being able to easily tap into many different skill sets.

Line and Staff Organizational Structure

Mid- and large-size firms commonly use a structure type that combines both the line and staff structures (Figure 5.3). For example, the company has a functional discipline structure with a creative group

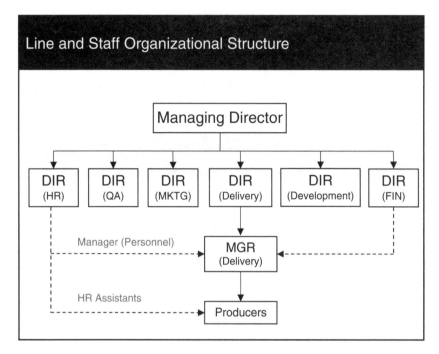

Figure 5.3   Line and staff organizational structure.

and a product management group, but they have expertise in healthcare, so they create a vertical for healthcare and dedicate a team of professionals to that vertical.

The removal of barriers between management levels allows for smooth and direct communication, making work processes in larger firms more flexible than other structures. This level relationship between line and staff managers, however, may cause disruption and conflict when attempting to coordinate across different groups. This structure emphasizes greater interaction at the top levels, where experience and knowledge are prized. The interaction between team members toward the bottom of the chart remains limited. Line and staff is not the most efficient communication structure. To ensure that firm values penetrate throughout the organization, upper-level management across all groups must place a greater emphasis on explicitly implementing programs that inculcate those values.

Divisional Organizational Structure

In a divisional structure (Figure 5.4), groups may be formed based on function, product, geographic territory, project, or a combination of two or more of these criteria.

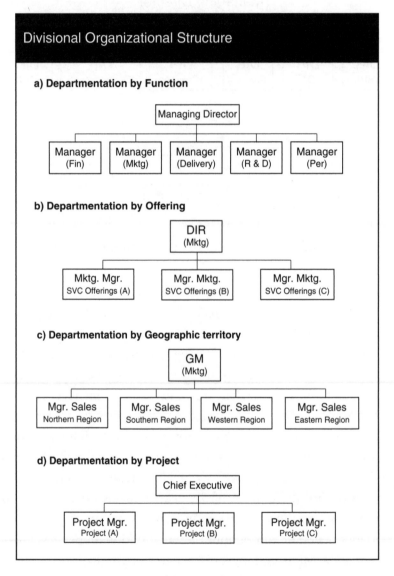

Figure 5.4   Divisional organizational structure.

For larger firms, a divisional structure works well because it allows an entire team to focus upon a single product or service, with a leadership structure that supports that group's major strategic objectives. This focus enables the leaders of that division to build a common culture and esprit de corps that contributes both to higher morale and a better knowledge of the division's portfolio. If your large firm values independence and innovation, separating into specific divisions with autonomy provides the opportunity to live this value in each different division.

Project Organizational Structure

In a project organizational structure (Figure 5.5), groups are divided by client or project. For example, everyone who works on the ABC

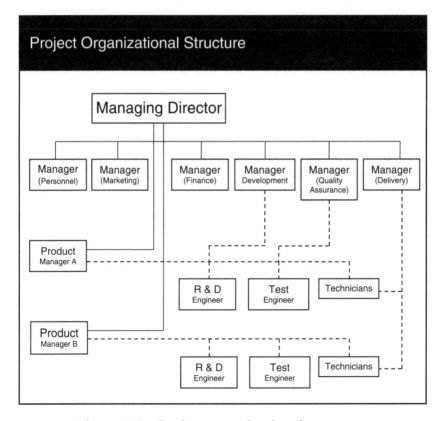

Figure 5.5 Project organizational structure.

account operates as a single entity, regardless of the role they play within the organization, and that account focused entity is a microcosm of the larger organization. Each self-contained group has its own creative team, finance managers, project managers, and so on. Project-based structures rely on the idea that groups are more efficient when all the people working on one project sit together. If your firm values efficiency and custom delivery, a project organization structure can enable both.

The type of organizational arrangement will be unique to each project. This customization ensures project work is completed in a disciplined way to achieve a specific goal. Getting senior leaders on the project working together is critical to prevent conflicts, which can significantly impact the delivery of the project.

These project teams are often created quickly from different parts of the organization. Alignment with your firm's purpose must take place from the first set of interactions within the new project team. This alignment can be a challenge when new members may have had little interaction with one another. For firms using project organization structures, the Three Keys need to be actively engaged in all areas of the firm, or the alignment at the project level will not materialize.

Matrix Organizational Structure

The matrix organizational structure (Figure 5.6) is designed to more effectively use teams of specialists from different functional areas in the organization to achieve results within a specific business offering. In the matrix organization, roles report to two people: one in the functional organization and one in the business offering organization. The matrix organization might be an alternative to the divisional structure for a large firm that values workflow integration and collaboration, as both are needed to succeed.

If changes within the group need to be made, it takes less time because the required experts are readily available to draw upon. However, the matrixed organization tends to have a larger number of senior managers, increasing overall costs and the potential for conflicts between leaders.

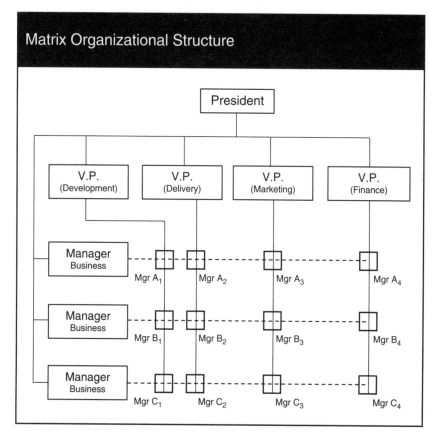

Figure 5.6 Matrix organizational structure.

These kinds of matrixed structures retain the organization's basic functional structure. This consistency allows for the rapid creation of efficient, large-scale project groups that utilize many team members of the organization's functional groups without disrupting or destroying the overall structure in the process.

Fewer Hands, Lower Risk

The organizational structure of the firm should optimize the workflow to efficiently satisfy the requirements of your clients. Choosing a structure should be based on identifying your clients' needs and the gaps you may find in the workflow to meet those needs. Follow the workflow through the organization. When a staff member has completed her work, where does it go next? Where does it go after that? Tracing the workflow setup creates a picture of the structure of your organization.

Different workflows yield different structures, so it is important to experiment. For example, a hypothetical workflow touches eighteen people before it is considered complete for the client. However, if you engineer the workflow in a different way, maybe only five people need to be involved. This is a more efficient workflow. The more hands that work touches, the more chances that quality will be compromised.

Different hierarchies within the organizational structure should also be explored. In flat organizations, each person on the management team may have many direct reports. As the company grows, managing an increasing number of direct reports becomes unsustainable. Leveraging other leaders to manage growing teams creates a more layered organization.

A Tale of Two Org Structures

When Investis and ZOG Digital merged, the two firms essentially combined two functional organizations. The new firm needed to blend two different sets of functional groups into one successfully integrated company. Investis builds corporate websites for our clients, but at the time, they weren't optimized for SEO. ZOG's SEO expertise added this capability. The new organization had to be developed, so the new workflow could include SEO as part of everything we do. If we didn't align the workflow to incorporate all the new expertise of ZOG, we were defeating the main reason for the merger.

We also had to adjust the firm's structure to adapt to a new selling structure and go-to-market approach. The concept of performance marketing now entered into our discussions about corporate website development. Development and engineering needs were then impacted by the changes to what we were now selling. Our org charts and workflows had to be modified to better meet the new requirements of our mission.

Is It Time to Change?

An organizational structure should never be viewed as permanent. The firm will come across a time when it needs to restructure to take on new or more aggressive goals. The following signposts from *Organizational Physics*[1] indicate that your organization's structure needs to be changed.

- The strategy has changed. The structure has not.
- You have strong individual departments and weak cross-functional coordination.
- The new business unit is failing to get traction.
- The CEO is a bottleneck.
- There's a lack of role clarity.
- Multiple senior-level hires haven't worked out.
- You've nailed the strategy. Now it's time to scale it.
- There's too much chaos.
- Short-range pressure is overpowering long-range development.
- You have high sales and low profits.

Is one or more of the above circumstances evidencing itself in your organization? If so, it may well be time to reorganize. The structure must evolve as your company evolves. During reorganizations, it becomes critical to provide your company with a unified vision for moving forward. As such, it is a great opportunity to reinforce your Three Keys. A study by McKinsey[2] suggests first to focus on longer-term strategic aspirations, and then assess the current situation of your firm. Think beyond the lines and boxes when selecting the new blueprint for your organization. A reorganization is a great time to put every role on the table and reassign according to the strengths, talents, and interests of your employees.

A reorganization also brings transitional risks that must be managed. Employees may *want change,* but most do not like *to change.* Once the new organizational structure is created, ensure that your executive team and department leaders communicate the changes clearly to their teams. Simply telling employees about the changes is not sufficient.

Create activities and programs that integrate the changes into the culture. A new organizational structure means a shift in how work gets accomplished and accompanying shifts in roles and responsibilities. These changes install a new mindset that must reflect the values of the firm and be actively lived in its culture.

Infuse Values throughout Your Firm

Ensuring that your firms' values are shared throughout the organization is critical regardless of the organizational structure chosen. Shared values encourage alignment throughout the firm. This alignment translates into profits, either through increased efficiencies, new clients, or hopefully, both. Failure to realize shared values and their benefits will ultimately splinter the organization.

In a small company, it is easier to make sure everyone in your organization lives the values and reflects them in the culture. A small, flat organization with most of the people reporting to a single leader enables that leader to "sing the music" every day and everyone will hear it. As the firm grows, the leadership team needs to understand the firm's mission and support its core values, and then a more complex organizational structure becomes feasible. But that original leader, founder, or CEO still sets the tone of the values.

For professional services firms, there is a growth point that creates significant challenges. This generally occurs when the organization reaches between seventy-five and one hundred people. With that many employees, even the most talented founder will find it impossible to control every aspect of the firm. The way forward calls for the founder to delegate and allow the various teams to manage themselves and get the work done.

At that point of growth, the firm's values will only be maintained if the leaders of the firm have been selected and developed to pass the values on to their subordinates. The founder must be willing to let go and leverage other leaders to instill the values throughout the organization.

The Org Chart Tells All

Don offers some great insight about using your org chart to determine if your structure supports your values:

Every box on the org chart needs to be associated with specific performance indicators. These indicators will measure how purposeful and how successful you are.

You can quickly see if a company lives the values they claim, such as technological leadership or commitment to clients, by looking at their organization structure. What does their technology group or account management team look like? Where does it fit into their overall organization?

I've heard organizations tout their technological superiority. Yet when I look at their org chart, there isn't a chief technology officer role. Or, if there is a lead technology role, it might be several layers below the executive level. That junior tech employee likely has no experience at the C-suite level. If this discrepancy is pointed out, these organizations often mumble and make excuses.

Investis Digital's simple organization structure implies clarity, one of our values. When we first meet with a client, we actually share our org chart; we want them to understand clearly how we operate. Investis Digital has a lean, flat structure with fewer levels of command and more people reporting to one manager. We can easily articulate how work moves around the organization.

In our specific case, our CTO reports at the uppermost level in the organization; this demonstrates that we value technology highly. If our goal is to help our clients be technologically savvy, we must show that our values and priorities align with that goal.

Organizational Design and the Three Keys

Your purpose and values help define your business; the organizational structure is the support system for the values and purpose. The structure is the roadmap for responsibility and accountability. It outlines the communication levels within the organization. All of these following considerations impact productivity and must be considered in thinking about organizational efficiency.

Leadership Impacts

Organizational structure cannot rectify problems caused by poor leadership. Even if the firm is organized in the most efficient manner, poor leadership will negate any positive impacts and the negative effects of bad leaders will eventually spread throughout the organization. Good leaders have the opposite effect, as efficient and intelligent decision-making can help improve productivity and raise overall efficiency.

Information Flows

In efficient and successful firms, information flows provide critical details about the state of the business, industry, or project. Decisions need to be made based on that information. An improperly designed organizational structure prevents critical information from traveling where it is ultimately necessary to make those decisions. The organizational structure needs to provide clear channels for information to flow, regardless of whether that information flows up, down, or across the org chart. Flaws in your organizational structure that reduce or limit communication need to be repaired to facilitate efficiency and effectiveness in decision making.

Bureaucracy Stifles

Bureaucracies that develop in organizations stifle creativity and hurt the productivity of good employees. Fresh, new ideas generated by employees are the innovation engine of any organization. This creativity encourages other employees and provides new ideas for senior leaders to act on. An organization structure that has become bureaucratic risks stagnation, unhappy employees, and dissatisfied clients.

Effective Communications Stimulates Growth

Identifying and eliminating communication "bottlenecks" is critical to keeping your organization on its proper growth path. For a growing firm, a structure that is designed to scale maintains corporate productivity during times of extreme growth and allows for improvements that will be necessary as the organization expands. Communication bottlenecks can happen at any point in the structure. Even though a bottleneck may seem insignificant at first, the firm's growth could quickly escalate the importance of correcting the issue.

What Can You Do?

The choice of organizational structure has a huge impact on your company's productivity, ability to deliver, and ultimately its profitability. The following action steps should be considered when looking to improve your company's organizational structure:

- Consider your values. Does your current organizational structure reflect them? Have you provided your staff with a unified vision to guide them?

- Look at your org chart. What roles are near the top? What roles are near the bottom? How does this org chart communicate your company's values? Consider whether your workflow needs to be changed to better reflect your company's values.
- Take a second look at your org chart and look for ways to minimize the number of people who work on a given project. How can you make your processes more efficient to improve quality?
- Consider the various organizational structures listed in this chapter, and whether your company needs to adapt its structure to better suit its needs. What structure are you currently operating in? Where would your company need to go next, as it grows?
- Meet with your company's leaders and ensure that everyone is on the same page regarding values. Can your leaders paraphrase the values that you want to infuse throughout the company? What are they doing to pass those values along to their team members?

With a solid organizational structure in place, the firm will be better prepared to purposefully meet your clients' needs and grow existing clients. The next chapter explores how your firm can better market its capabilities and take advantage of the Three Keys to procure new clients.

Notes

1. https://organizationalphysics.com/2019/02/26/the-top-10-signs-its-time-to-change-your-organizational-structure/
2. https://www.mckinsey.com/business-functions/organization/our-insights/getting-organizational-redesign-right

6

Messages Matter: Marketing and Communications

Saying hello does not have an ROI. It's about building relationships.
—*Gary Vaynerchuk*, Jab, Jab, Jab, Right Hook: How to Tell Your Story in a Noisy Social World

Put simply, marketing is the process of attracting people to your company's services.

However, marketing as a process is not simple. It's quite complex and these days it is evolving very rapidly. Marketing relates to all aspects of your business—internally and externally. It manifests itself from the top of the organization to the bottom—from the CEO to the receptionist and all the salespeople, line employees, and middle managers in between. Internally, every employee has a responsibility to infuse their

109

work product with your firm's brand foundation. The leader who bears the torch for this integration, and sets the standard for your brand foundation, is the CEO.

Marketing happens through understanding your ideal customer's interests. You arrive at this apprehension by listening to your customers. For larger firms, market research and analysis will add deeper layers of understanding. Still, firms of any size have the ability to listen and hear what their customers want through thoughtful conversation. Once you understand your ideal customer, marketing's job is to communicate about your service in a way that resonates directly with them. If the communication is done successfully, the prospect begins a journey that ultimately leads them to become a paying customer with a long-term, repeating relationship.

Throughout this book, we show how the Three Keys—purpose, values, and story—will drive your success to new and exciting levels. Marketing is where your story makes its impact on your customers. It is a good time for you to review your brand foundation. All the groundwork laid will go to waste if that foundation does not fully express itself in the act of marketing.

Marketing Today

There was a time when new business generation was based primarily on referrals. Clients came to you based on what they heard about you from other customers. This was pre-internet, when learning about a product or service was typically done face to face. Given the challenges of personally reaching every possible customer, existing customers sending new customers your way was common. In the past, general name recognition generated by advertising might also generate new customers. This was a hit-or-miss endeavor captured nicely by this old aphorism: "I'm pretty sure 50 percent of my advertising is working. I just don't know which 50 percent."

Today is different. Today, your marketing messages rely on *content*. Content in marketing isn't product information, though it may contain such information. Content isn't static; it needs to be agile. Content, in its myriad forms (more on that later), is where the process of marketing happens today.

Different audiences consume content, and therefore your messages and stories, in different ways. The number of platforms, styles of engagement, and methods of consumption is mind numbing. Figuring it all out so your company can be successful is what makes marketing complex. Your message will be simple, but how that story gets told will not be.

Agility is the key: planning, testing, and adjusting in different ways to attract your audience and nurture the relationship until they become a client and then evolve them into a raving fan of your brand.

In contrast to the old way of pushing out messages, brands today must engage. You must ask questions and share relevant content that is informed by the brand foundation developed with the Three Keys. Engagement is how the consumer builds an active relationship with your brand. And never forget, you're always building a relationship with your clients.

The ability to listen to your clients and to what others say about you is part of the engagement formula. Listening has always been crucial, but the power of the internet means that the collection of data—and specifically data showing what customers want and think about your service—is now possible for every business. Later in this chapter we will go into detail about the power of data in marketing.

Marketing theorists have coined two generic terms to describe the two basic approaches to telling your story: inbound and outbound. The great debate in marketing is about which approach is more effective. For most organizations, both are needed, and the role of marketing is to integrate these two approaches in a way that successfully reaches your audience and converts them from non-customers to customers. We'll discuss these approaches later in this chapter.

Investis Digital's Marketing Journey

Historically, Investis had always struggled when it came to a cohesive marketing approach. The role of marketing had really been a "top of funnel" approach in building name recognition. This had worked fairly well in the more well-established London office, but not so much in New York, where we were starting from scratch and had no name recognition.

Yet, after five years, many changes in CMOs, and a comprehensive rebrand campaign, the situation began to improve. We were still strong in the UK and had built some name recognition in the United States and hired a first-class CMO who realized our approach should now be more "middle of the funnel." By this, I mean acquiring leads that are further down the funnel. They know what they want and are looking for someone who has insights into their issues. It's all about data.

We are now beginning to see benefits from our reinvigorated marketing approach. As we continue to bring solutions forward that are grounded in data and provide clients with the insights they are looking for, we become increasingly successful.

Now that you have a better idea of how we view marketing, let's dive into how it relates to the Three Keys—purpose, values, and story.

How the Three Keys Affect Marketing

Marketing is how the world hears about your purpose. It is where your values, your firm's "personality," is shown to the world. Marketing is sharing your story. Marketing is *not* telling people what you think they want to hear; it's about showing people who you really are.

That's why the Three Keys create a supportive framework and become the bedrock of your marketing. The Three Keys guide you in *how* to communicate to your desired customers.

Creating an externally facing, purpose-led brand requires the development of the brand foundation. When your Three Keys are defined, each one serves to attract others who believe what you believe. Actively using the Three Keys in your brand consistently attracts those who are aligned with your purpose. Successful marketers weave their values, mission, and vision into the story.

Marketing guided by the Three Keys attracts new clients with aligned beliefs who connect emotionally. From there, you begin to earn trust. If you take the time to determine where your alignment with the client is, it becomes an anchor for the relationship. If you use that connection to solve a problem your client actually has, as opposed to the one they think they have, you earn trust. With that trust and alignment, they'll want you to provide a solution for them.

When you satisfy your customers, they are happy. It is natural for people to share their excitement about something they love. They don't keep that excitement to themselves. Happy customers reward your firm by telling others who are similarly aligned about you. Then the cycle repeats with those evangelists sharing their experience with others who share your values, thus helping to grow your business by creating receptive new potential customers.

Fran Hears an Echo

One of the things I listen for in customer conversations is the echo of my firm's values. I want to hear that prospects have alignment with some part of our Three Keys. Our purpose is helping our customers break through the noise and Get Noticed. I still remember the very first time Advantage's Three Keys came back to me through a prospective client. We had just started putting purpose-based content out into the world when a potential customer called me and said, "Hi, you don't know me, but your client Judah told me that you were the agency that could help me Get Noticed." That was the first time someone I didn't know had picked up the phone and said that; he had my full attention.

The caller continued, "I explained my problem to Judah. He said, 'I have the perfect agency to help you.' He told me how you helped him accomplish more than he expected. Not only was he happy, he was very confident I would be, too." I listened intently to make sure I understood his issues. What I heard was that a potential client had received my purpose-based content, and that client knew how to use it to connect someone's need to my ability to solve a challenge. Just like that, I was able to put content into the world (actual simple, repeatable words that someone could explain) and it would come back to me if there was alignment. There was already trust between Judah, my existing client and the potential new client. This is indeed how an echo works.

For the first time in this conversation, I heard the Advantages Three Keys—purpose, values, and story—coming back to me like an echo. This was in the beginning; we regularly experience this echo today.

What Does Purpose Have to Do with It?

In an article by Accenture, "To Affinity and Beyond: From Me to We, the Rise of the Purpose-Led Brand,"[1] Larry Fink, the CEO of investment firm BlackRock, Inc., said, "The public expectations of your company have never been greater. . . Every company must not only deliver financial performance, but also show how it makes a positive contribution to society. Without a sense of purpose, no company, either public or private, can achieve its full potential."

Given BlackRock's position as the largest investment firm on the planet, with $6.8 trillion in assets under management, Fink's comment underscores the shift that has occurred in the way the world thinks about business and its role in society.

The article goes on to mention the success that Unilever, the global consumer products company, has had incorporating purpose:

Unilever has seen, first-hand, the tangible value of making purpose a core driver of growth and differentiation. Nearly half of its top 40 brands focus on sustainability. These "Sustainable Living" brands, including Knorr, Dove, and Lipton, are good for society. They are also good for Unilever—growing 50 percent faster than the company's other brands and delivering more than 60 percent of the company's growth.

Purpose isn't specifically about sustainability or social responsibility. In fact, purpose isn't always "save the world." The reason for identifying your purpose is to find those clients with whom you align.

Accenture's research reinforces the critical need to understand the underlying part of your brand foundation that causes clients to trust your brand. When trust is broken because you're not really living the values you say you stand for, it will cost you. In today's age of transparency, watchdog groups, and social media, a small slipup has the ability to quickly become viral and you risk losing your carefully built brand reputation—all the more reason that *everyone* in your organization must live and align with your Three Keys. If your marketing materials—from your website to your print ads to your social media feed—tout "Embrace Diversity," yet your firm and client base is homogeneous, it won't take long for that disconnect to become obvious to your team, your clients, and eventual prospects. The clients who have hired you because they align with your values will think twice about their choice. Likewise, potential employees will not consider your firm; you will be eliminated early in the process. If "Embrace Diversity" is one of your values, use your story to show how your staff and clients represent this value, and talk about why it's important to you.

Story is the opportunity to demonstrate that you live the purpose and values you speak. There are as many ways to deliver your story as there are stories, so explore them all, from content marketing to events and everything in between. If you don't tell your story, others will fill in the blanks and make up their own story about you.

A Tale of Two Clients

Don worked with two different clients about a decade ago, each of which faced financial trouble during hard economic times. He tells their tales and the predictable outcomes:

Professional Services Firm A: Lies Can Kill You

Only the CEO and a few key team members knew the financial trouble Firm A faced. They hid the truth from the staff, denying the team the opportunity to rally and come together in difficult times. Resources were drying up, client deliverables and deadlines were missed, and no explanation was given. Direct questions from employees went unanswered, leaving them to make excuses to clients—or simply tell the truth that they didn't know what was happening. It didn't take long for confused employees and clients to lose trust in Firm A. Both started leaving the company, which eventually closed its doors. The irony of the story is that Firm A's brand foundation states: "Shared values guide how we go about our business. They are weaved into our processes, reviews, and the way we conduct ourselves daily." When they forgot to live their values, their business failed.

Professional Services Firm B: Honesty Is the Best Policy

The CEO at Firm B gathered the employees in the conference room and laid the situation out on the table: things were bad, the economy was down (this was 2008). New clients were few and existing clients were reducing their requests. Appreciative of the CEO's honesty, the team rallied: they agreed to a 15 percent pay cut to support the firm's recovery—better a lower-paying job than no job at all. They worked rotating four-day weeks when the workload was slower. Clients received their work as always. The firm rebounded and everyone was rewarded personally and financially. No one lost their job, and the firm continued to grow, with low employee churn and higher client retention rates. One of their values was "Communicate Clearly and Courageously." The CEO was guided by the firm's Three Keys and lived to tell the tale.

Accenture isn't alone in laying out the case for purpose. *Harvard Business Review* published "The Business Case for Purpose," which we have mentioned elsewhere in this book. Kantar Consulting released its "Purpose 2020" report that surveyed over fifteen thousand consumers and six hundred senior marketing executives and determined that "purposeful positioning" was a leading driver of marketing success.

In the next section, we talk a bit about how specific marketing activities relate to the Three Keys.

How to Market: A Tactical Discussion

Paradoxically, thanks to technology, clients today are both harder and easier to find. Harder because your audience spends its time in many places that it never used to, and you need to find them. Data gathered through the internet, mobile devices, social media, and a plethora of other channels provide the ability to discover them, see what they are doing, and then target messages and channels to reach them effectively.

As mentioned previously, today's marketing activities can be divided into two segments. One is outbound. This is the realm of what could be called traditional marketing and includes advertising and direct mail, which are basically activities where marketers send out messages in the hope that consumers will respond. Outbound is a numbers game based on percentages. With outbound, you are searching to find someone who needs your services. There are numerous tactics, besides advertising, that fit into this category.

The other approach is inbound. Inbound is defined by programs that successfully connect with clients and drive them to your firm. Customers seek you out instead of the other way around. They seek things that interest them and align with their values. This means that how and where you tell your story helps those potential clients and employees find you. For example, a potential client may search "socially responsible trustworthy accountant" because it's important to her to work with an accountant who is both trustworthy (obviously) and who perhaps does pro bono work for nonprofits. If your story includes details about your work with your local Habitat for Humanity group, you're one step closer to aligning with that potential client.

Inbound really starts to address insights. People come to you based on what you know. This could be from content you've created, such as articles or social media posts, or from using improved optimization in organic search. These tactics may or may not overtly sell your service. They could discuss common challenges your customers face or demonstrate a similarity or value alignment on social media such as a charity event or cultural interaction. Inbound has advantages because your potential client has taken the initiative to find you for some specific reason and is well on their way to becoming a truly qualified prospect all on their own.

If marketing, whether inbound or outbound, is derived from the purposeful brand foundation created by the Three Keys, the efforts to make that connection will be much more successful. The recipient of the outbound message or the seeker for the inbound action will have identified you as a possible provider because something about your firm resonated with them. It is highly unlikely it will be just because of the service you sell. In professional services, where your offering is differentiated by service and ideas, this is particularly true.

One of the reasons why we will talk about the death of solution selling (Chapter 7) has to do with the overload of information available about you online. If you're not going deeper and providing an insight based on expertise that the client can't find elsewhere, you're not going to make the sale.

In their "State of Inbound 2018"[2] report, Hubspot identified a number of trends worth considering in the inbound versus outbound marketing debate. According to Hubspot's research, 68 percent of inbound marketers are more likely to believe that their efforts are effective, versus 48 percent of outbound who believe in the effectiveness of their efforts. This effectiveness translates into perceived higher ROI for their activities, with 46 percent of marketers noting a higher ROI and 59 percent of marketers surveyed claiming higher quality leads for their sales teams.

HubSpot's research also surfaced some interesting data that provides support for these survey results:

- B2B companies that blogged over eleven times per month received three times more traffic than B2B companies that blogged once or less per month.
- 47 percent of buyers view three to five pieces of the company's content before talking with a sales representative.
- 96 percent of B2B buyers want content that has input from industry thought leaders.
- 66 percent of marketers see lead generation benefits with social media after only six hours a week dedicated to social media marketing.

Creating valuable, relevant, and helpful content is the linchpin for inbound marketing. It needs to be truthful, authentic content or critical insights that your audience will connect with. Your audience is searching for content. Potential customers want great content from leaders and experts they can trust. With great content, you position your firm as an expert who's available for them when they need you.

Key Tactics

Search Engine Optimization

According to HubSpot, 61 percent of marketers said improving their SEO and growing their organic presence was the top marketing priority heading into 2019. When searching with Google, most users are intent on finding search results that are not paid, but rather surface due to the various algorithms Google creates to identify highly reliable and popular information on that search term.

Mobile

Nearly everyone has a mobile device. Executives are pressed for time and mobile-based marketing interactions with your firm are more than likely the norm rather than the exception. You need to make sure your efforts are optimized for mobile.

Mobile devices have also provided a real-time local flavor for marketing interactions. Professional services can often be a location-driven purchasing decision and there are opportunities to engage and learn about your customers at the local and hyper-local level.

Social Media

Though consumer brands are famous for using social media, B2B customers are also on social media. In addition, you should rely on your employees to be brand ambassadors through their own social media channels. Encourage sharing of relevant firm content on their LinkedIn, Facebook, or Instagram accounts.

Your content needs to be findable in a variety of locations, not just via search.

Account-Based Marketing

The concept of account-based marketing takes outbound marketing to an ultra-narrow focus, keeping your company in front of the specific set of accounts that interest you. This results in a regular stream of interaction and personalized content that addresses clients' particular issues.

Don't forget print or events. These "old school" experiences in the customer journey—something your customer can touch, feel, and connect with, such as print and in-person events—are still important to the dimension of your relationship. Today's digital to print systems allow for creating hardcopy materials in an economical manner.

Every expert has an opinion about different tactics. Marketing leaders have a dizzying array of choices about how to tactically go about their job. Pros and cons exist for every tactic. Decisions about which to use and how should be based on the concepts brought up in the Three Keys. Are you living up to the brand foundation identified by the Three Keys? Are your tactical marketing choices in alignment with that brand foundation? Your Three Keys will impact the choices you make in your marketing tactics.

It is not a question of one or the other; find the best combination that fits for your strategy and use story to deliver the messages that align with your purpose and resonate with the potential clients.

There is a final tactical consideration before we move into data. Learning through experimenting is probably the biggest part of marketing tactics today—testing to find what works and what does not, then doing more of what does work. You may have heard of "fail quickly" or "growth hacking"—terms borrowed from software developers and entrepreneurs. Rather than working on something until it is perfect and then releasing it to the world, practice trial and error. You want to gain insight into your customer so you can offer insight. Sometimes tests fail to bring the results you seek but are still valuable—you learned that the tactic tested did not evoke the desired connection or that you asked the wrong questions. With this new information in hand, it is time to try a different marketing tactic.

Testing is far more cost-effective in the long run, because listening to your customer is much easier to do today. With today's technology, any of these tactics has, at its core, an opportunity to collect terabytes of relevant data, which can be analyzed to learn more about your potential clients. The information gleaned from the data enables more tailored marketing efforts, which more successfully share your story and engage and attract more closely aligned clients. Test in smaller markets, get feedback, modify, and then test again.

Data: Opportunity or Overload?

According to a 2014 GlobalDMA article, "The Global Review of Data-Driven Marketing and Advertising," "Technology is maturing, information is available in abundance, and a new corporate mandate—create actionable insights from data, big and small, that drive value for brands and consumers alike—has propelled the marketer into a powerful new role as an agent for change."[3]

Data is the biggest game-changing opportunity for marketing and sales since the internet went mainstream less than twenty-five years ago. There is more data than ever before. From first party to third party, data has the potential to be the most valuable marketing resource because you now can lead with insights, not intuition. Data becomes actionable. This change has been critical in professional services. The value our firms provide to a client is the intelligence wrapper that goes around the data.

Once upon a time, marketing and sales leaders relied on gut feelings and insights from mailed surveys and focus groups. That took a lot of time and money, and even then, it was difficult to truly understand which marketing efforts were driving the biggest return in both the short and the long run.

Now we have an abundance of data that gives marketers the right insights and information to create smart, scalable, and repeatable marketing programs that drive your audiences through the full funnel from awareness to conversion.

How Investis Digital Uses Data

Don shares how Investis Digital uses data in its sales and marketing approach:

Performance marketing is very measurable. We collect data about potential clients and then use it for targeted "outbound" marketing. We take a prospect's website and provide feedback based on the data we collect, such as how it ranks for specific keywords or how the terms are converting. We benchmark this information and let the prospect know how they are performing and how Investis Digital can assist them. Our staff isn't worried about being replaced by a computer or robot, however.

(continued)

Leveraging data requires a human-friendly filter over the information to make sense of it. Done correctly, these data-based insights help build more compelling narratives and create incredible and measurable experiences.

Marketers now can leverage data and tools (such as Think with Google) to quickly and easily:

- Identify trends on what people are engaging and searching for to inform marketing efforts across all channels
- Explore real-time data to glean insights about consumer research, shopping actions, and purchase behaviors to make more strategic decisions about marketing campaigns and ad spending
- Use demographic data to enable more context in marketing efforts and targeting
- Use trends from one marketing channel to inform another (i.e., use data from our digital channels to inform our web copy, campaigns, events, and so on)

These insights allow companies to make smarter, more informed, and more impactful marketing efforts that drive engagement, awareness, and performance.

The Chief Marketing Officer Is Dead, Long Live the CMO

If you look at the org chart, the CMO today is not what it used to be. The chief marketer joined the C-Suite in the 1980s. Back then, the CMO was the creative and strategy lead who led another team of junior marketing executives, who in turn led production teams. Today, the role has completely changed. Along with those big budgets, the freewheeling days of the CMO, as well as their Madison Avenue counterparts, are over.

The CMO is being tasked with a greater responsibility to make marketing a revenue driver and an enterprise-wide function that captures ever-increasing shares of their clients' wallets. This expanded role has come with a change in expected skill set. In an interview for *Marketing* in July 2019, Anindya Dasgupta, Fonterra's former global CMO, commented that today's CMOs are required to be "extremely analytical while being highly creative."[4] In some cases, there is also a change in title. Chief Growth Officer, Chief Brand Officer, Customer Experience Officer, and many others have been introduced. Coca-Cola consolidated marketing into the executive role of Chief Growth Officer, held by Francisco Crespo. His responsibilities extend to corporate strategy and retail relationships. He was quoted in an *AdAge* article published in July 2019 saying, "Bringing the disciplines under a single leader helped Coke ensure that building brands was not only creating strong preference and equity but also translating that equity into revenue and margin growth."[5]

The CMO's title may be changing but every firm still has a leader who is responsible for the objective of marketing the company's services. Without that leader, there is no one accountable. And without accountability, there will be no results. Either way, if you are a tactical, creative-focused marketing executive who cannot understand customer data—either collection or analysis of it—your days leading marketing are numbered.

Small and mid-sized companies face even bigger challenges. Strategy is expensive. Many of these firms outsource strategy to some degree and hire an "acting CMO" with some sharp skill sets, but not usually in all disciplines. Then they hire freelancers to execute the strategy. These freelancers often don't know how to connect the brand foundation to the creative. They need to be educated; they also need to align. Whether you hire a firm or build an internal team, your creative team needs to understand the alignment to your Three Keys.

Regardless of size, the firm still needs someone who thinks strategically about marketing. Does it make sense to outsource strategy? Wouldn't it make more sense to outsource creative and have someone internally who can strategically drive the creative? It's pretty easy to outsource a social media manager, harder to outsource a leader who will understand and guide your message. Someone has to provide that strategic guidance: the CMO.

What Should CMOs Do?

The CMO today does have a vital strategic role to play in today's professional services company. It is the role of the CMO to let the market know that your firm is on top of the issues that your clients are facing today and have solutions based on insights to address these issues.

Be the expert on the firm's customers.

If the customers sit at the center of the organization, the CMO's most critical responsibility is to engage and serve them with a profoundly intricate comprehension of all their needs. As noted earlier, this requires knowledge of data and analytics.

Learn how to speak CEO and board-level language.

At the board level, the preferred language is financial accountability. Essentially, marketing needs to be a line role where the leader has to have accountability for revenue and profit—not just spend. The CMO's authority has to have a positive financial impact. The days of asking for more marketing dollars and wondering how to justify it since it's viewed by the Board as an "expense" are over.

Get data savvy along with all the fun creative stuff you may like to do.

Earlier in the chapter, we discuss all the data and analytics that have come along with the rise of the internet and proliferation of technology. As a marketing leader, the CMO is required to understand how to use all that data to produce results and convey insights to C-Suite colleagues. But don't forget why you went into marketing in the first place—creativity is still a must-have for marketing leaders.

What Can You Do?

Though the marketing world is complex and the role of the CMO is evolving, it's not a time to shrink into the corner. Regardless of what it's called, how it's done, and the title of the executive who leads it, to paraphrase Forrest Gump, "Marketing happens," and that should be the focus.

- Create a narrative—your story—that supports your brand, your purpose, and your values. Our brains remember stories twenty-two times more than facts alone. Think about different ways to tell yours:
  - Create an experience that aligns with your purpose and values and that clients can join.
  - Use visuals—this is especially important in the image-driven digital age.
  - Involve your clients—testimonials and social sharing turn your clients into ambassadors for your brand, which is the most effective marketing available today.
- Find an agency that understands the journey of a purpose-led firm.
- Don't ignore the importance of aligning marketing with your Three Keys.

- Invest in data capabilities and leverage the information you gather to speak to your clients and offer insight, based on their needs.

If you take the Three Keys to heart in your marketing strategy and filter all your communications tactics through them, you'll likely be attracting a lot of potential new clients. The next chapter helps you understand how values-based professional services firms truly serve clients.

Notes

1. https://www.accenture.com/_acnmedia/thought-leadership-assets/pdf/accenture-competitiveagility-gcpr-pov.pdf#zoom=50
2. http://www.stateofinbound.com
3. http://www.globaldma.com/resources/global-review-data-driven-marketing-advertising/
4. https://www.marketing-interactive.com/the-changing-cmo-title-will-we-see-the-role-as-we-know-it-being-wiped-out-soon/
5. https://adage.com/article/cmo-strategy/why-more-brands-are-ditching-cmo-position/2183166

7 | Clients Matter

> *"There is only one boss. The customer. And he can fire everybody in the company from the chairman on down, simply by spending his money somewhere else."*
> —*Sam Walton, founder of Walmart and Sam's Club*
> *retail stores*

Clients are the inspiration and livelihood of any professional services organization. Yet, so often, as the provider of the services, we lose sight of this fact. How many times have you thought, "If it weren't for the clients, I'd really enjoy this business." If you don't enjoy client service, you have no business being in a professional services firm.

The Three Keys, as detailed throughout the book, align your firm's purpose—its mission and vision—to a set of values. The communication of these values and purpose through a compelling story leads to the magic of attracting like-minded employees whose increased productivity and loyalty deliver great things for your clients. Clients have been likewise attracted to your firm by shared values, as well as terrific results. In this chapter, we will focus on those clients, both before the selling and during delivery of your services. First, let's look at how clients buy services.

Purpose before Services

In a new client situation, building credibility is an active process. A good sales team must know how to listen for and understand a prospective client's unique situation. In these initial interactions, it is critical that your team communicates your company's purpose. Clients don't buy what you do; they buy why you do it. For that reason, early in the sales process, it is important not to focus on selling your services; instead, focus on identifying similar values and making the emotional connection that earns trust.

Fran's Challenge or Opportunity?

When Investis Digital approached Fran for a possible project, they were confident they knew exactly what they wanted and they had a super-tight timeline. Advantages is a highly detailed agency that starts at the core with its clients. Even working with a supplied, fully baked creative brief and a thirty-day target was hardly their norm. Fran was passionate about the opportunity she saw in this new company that Don was creating. Despite the constraints, she appreciated the challenge they were having, and felt compelled to help them unify. Her process was going to challenge his expectations, so she needed to earn trust. Fran vividly described her passion for the project and delivered a sensible proposal. Her purpose-driven approach aligned with her company's purpose and demonstrated that she had some skin in the game—meaning she was taking a risk that her work might not ultimately win out. Her goal in the sales process was to establish trust and create a fair engagement that would deliver the greatest chance for success.

The client always wants to know who you are and what differentiates you from the competition. You explore and demonstrate alignment by sharing your purpose and values, then use story to build emotional connection. You have to introduce yourself and weave your values into your introduction before your sales pitch. Make an emotional connection based on common beliefs at the beginning. This connection will go a long way to establish a trusting relationship. Lead the conversation by stating three values your company believes and the purpose you stand for. Then you are able to explain how they manifest in the high-quality service you deliver. Reiterate the issues you hear facing the potential client, identify with them, and show how you can provide a solution.

New clients help you accelerate your growth; existing clients keep the engine running. It can be easy to forget the importance of retaining clients. A steady current revenue stream may seem to make the business stable. However, where will the business stand if a large client leaves, and your revenue drops suddenly? That lost revenue must be covered in the short term, and substantial additional effort must be spent to find a new client to replace the one that left.

The benefits of prioritizing investments in existing clients are clear. Existing clients are more cost-effective to retain than new clients are to land. They know you, and you know them; the working and personal relationships become more engaged and authentic over time. Both client and provider are familiar with the expectations and workflow, which means that the client is more likely to have an experience they find valuable. Deepening the relationships with your current clients and serving them better helps to ensure their retention. With these stronger relationships, your firm is likely to secure their word-of-mouth recommendation, which will help you gain new clients. The best approach for gaining new clients, ironically, is to give gold star treatment to your current clients.

SuperPleasing

Over the past twenty-five years, few concepts in how professional services firms think about current clients have withstood the test of time like David Maister's Client SuperPleasing, described in detail in his book *How to Market a Professional Services Firm*. Following is a brief excerpt of Maister's thinking:

- "Instead of spending time with clients at a social or business event, or in 'marketing meetings,' spend it on the project you're working with them on and do an even better job than you would have done otherwise."
- "In short, spend your time and money in any way you can think of so that the client not only thinks you did a great job for them (which should be the baseline) but that they think you've done the best job of any service provider they've hired."
- "You need to focus on the high priority ones who have the potential to give you lots of new business, or strong referrals to other potential clients."
- "But if you superplease them like this it's the strongest way of getting them to buy more and to recommend you with enthusiasm."

How do you do that with the Three Keys? Communicate your purpose, determine if your values align, and focus on solving your clients' problems.

Align with Purpose

The common denominator in retaining clients, developing current client relationships, and setting yourself up for securing new clients is the alignment of people through purposeful interactions. But what are purposeful interactions? Entrepreneur.com states, "Selling with purpose is more about finding a good fit than fitting your products and services to their needs."[1] We couldn't agree more.

In an aptly titled article, "Do You Have a Purpose or Do You Just Sell Stuff?"[2] Lisa Earle McLeod writes about the Noble Sales Purpose (NSP). She cites a study showing that purpose-driven salespeople outsell product-driven salespeople. There's a reason that purpose is the first of the Three Keys. When purpose is the foundation for everything your company does, bad sales behavior is minimized, even eliminated, and motivation increases. This creates an organic lever for increasing sales.

When the internal conversations revolve around purpose, values, and making a difference, the right aligned clients will identify with that energy. If your beliefs align, your message will resonate with them. If the internal sales conversations at your firm focus only on your fees and potential profitability of clients, that message will also end up reaching your clients.

In a study issued by EY Beacon Institute and *Harvard Business Review*,[3] 85 percent of the 474 business executives surveyed indicated they strongly agree that they are more likely to recommend a company with a strong purpose. Further, 80 percent of those executives also strongly agreed that a company with a shared purpose will have greater customer loyalty.

Align at a Higher Level

If a potential client asks what your firm does, do not say "branding and marketing" or "public relations" or blandly state whatever form of professional service you provide. Instead, use your purpose as a point of entry. Ask what the client's organization does and what they're trying to achieve.

In conversations with prospects, customize the questions you ask. It is extremely important to find out what is actually going on with the client. Cookie-cutter sales questions do not achieve the necessary level of detail. From there, discover what they are committed to. What does success really look like for them? Then paint a vivid picture for the prospect. At this point in the conversation, it cannot be about your specific capabilities or expertise.

When prospecting new clients, the initial process is about building a relationship between two organizations that align on the same beliefs, nothing more. For example, maybe global clean water is important to you and sustainability is a value of your firm. It is possible to align with potential clients who seek to deliver products or services based on clean water and sustainability. In this example, initial alignment is quite apparent. However, when values are less overt or tangible, it will take more relationship-building to determine alignment.

If you sell services to the market just by stating your differences from the competition, the opportunity to talk about what you stand for is rarely given. When you speak to a client about what your firm stands for and combine that with the potential client's vision, alignment occurs at a higher level. Speak to what the client wants to accomplish in the world, because if you can align with the client, chances are you can consistently help them accomplish their goals through delivering different services year in and year out. In a climate of constant change your clients' alignment with your Three Keys helps create lifetime relationships.

Bungee Cord or Umbilical Cord

Fran has a great analogy about building successful long-term client relationships. She calls it the difference between a bungee cord and an umbilical cord. An umbilical cord suggests a relationship of dependence, often with negative or controlling overtones. In child-rearing, when a parent fails to "cut the cord," it's not seen as a positive. In the same way, you want to have healthy creative relationships with your clients where you are pulled and attracted to different projects because they make sense creatively, strategically, and profitably. Hence the bungee: your clients should be free to expand their reach and have the safety of reaching back to engage you. Ultimately, it creates a more exhilarating and rewarding client relationship.

When you focus on a company's purpose, vision, and mission, you can talk about their direction and what they want to achieve—but only if you know how to have that conversation. Such a conversation requires getting vulnerable with the people involved. You have to learn what they deeply wish to achieve with their project or business or life. Your vulnerability allows them to open up and share these bigger-picture ideas. Once you align on a shared belief and have identified an opportunity to provide a solution, you've begun to earn their trust. You build credibility when you deliver on your promises, but you earn trust through shared beliefs.

Commonality provides a point of entry on shared values. For example, you buy a red hat and think no one in the world wears red hats. Then, the day you wear your red chapeau down the streets of New York, you see six people in a seven-block radius wearing red hats. You may no longer feel so unique, but at the same time, you are recognizing people who identify with you and have the same appreciation for red hats.

When looking for new prospects, find some commonality from the first conversation with that prospect. Do this and there now exists a point of connection. If you don't look for it, you won't know that it is there.

Understand the Problem as the Client Sees It

The word "services" often distracts professional services firms from the true purpose of the firm: to solve clients' problems. *Professional solutions firm* is more accurate. Your focus should be on providing a complete answer to your clients' problems, not simply choosing a service from your portfolio to extend to them. As you learn how they communicate and think about their issues, you can offer appropriate solutions to their problems.

However, fail to listen closely to your clients and you run the risk of disappointing them, even if you deliver what they asked for. If what you deliver does not solve the problem the client actually has, your client will likely place the fault with you. Their disappointment will strain the relationship.

Ask clients about the cause and effect of the solution they seek. Help them define the experience that will happen if you implement the solution they ask for. Understand the journey the particular service will take. To do this, ask framing questions that lead with curiosity:

- Tell me more about . . .
- I'm curious how this worked.
- Did you ever think about it this way . . .

Get validation of the problem as the client sees it. You can then align with what they're saying and propose something like, "I understand we have this opportunity. This is what you want to accomplish and here's how I see us getting there." Ask the client to paraphrase what you just told them, in their own words. This reiteration will confirm that they see your path to the solution. If the client says that it is not what they're looking for, you have an opportunity to continue the conversation. You must be a keen listener.

You and your client are taking a journey together. Get to know each other and understand how you each communicate so that you can deliver a solution that your client will find valuable.

The RFP Conundrum

Generally speaking, pursuing the dreaded "request for proposal" (RFP) can be a challenging way for professional services firms to go after business. If your work involves the need to respond to RFPs—many public entities and nonprofits have specific requirements for winning their business—you need to understand the values and build relationships with the specific organization before that RFP comes out. The trust developed by getting to know the originator of the RFP will actually enable you to craft the RFP in such a way that it plays to your specific strengths and helps you win the business. If you're not willing to invest the time and energy to build these relationships, the pursuit of RFPs will likely be futile.

Flip the Funnel

The traditional sales and marketing prospect funnel is a Y-shaped graphic. At the top of the "funnel" are hundreds (if not thousands) of potential customers; as they pass through the funnel you end up with a handful of actual customers. Theory and misguided logic would have us believe that if you increase the size of the funnel, you will increase your number of customers. It takes a lot of time, resources, and energy to grow that funnel. There is a better alternative.

Flip the funnel on its side, so it becomes your megaphone! (See Figure 7.1.) Now concentrate on what you are projecting out into the world. Your purpose, of course, is the "one thing" that you can shout into your megaphone. Rather than casting a wider net, if you project your purpose clearly and loudly, you will attract fewer but more qualified clients who align with your values. Why? These clients respond to what you are projecting, like a bat following an echo. Research has shown that humans are instinctively drawn to other humans who sound like they do. Companies can act similarly. Your firm will attract clients who are more aligned with its values and more eager to work with you, as opposed to a competitor, if they hear your one thing—your purpose. As you focus on customers who echo your values, these steady clients become the ambassadors of your brand, creating an indirect sales force touting your values.

In his book *Crossing the Chasm*, Geoffrey Moore beautifully lays this out. He writes specifically about products, but given the changes in the way we communicate today, his point applies to services as well (Figure 7.2).

FLIP THE FUNNEL: Make a Megaphone!

Figure 7.1   Forget the funnel. Project your message through your megaphone.

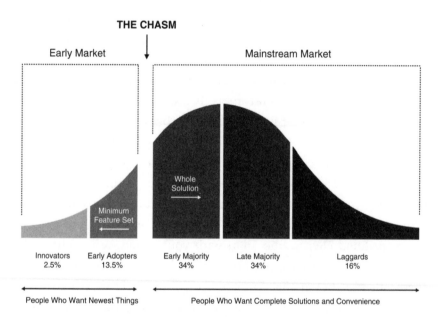

Figure 7.2   Changes in communication have influenced how people adopt products and services.

In the beginning, only the innovators talk about you. These are the people who want the newest, most recent version of a gadget (or service); they wait on line the day it is released. The innovators are the ones who tell you how the product or service can be improved. When you address those comments, they then tell the early adopters to try your product or service. When enough early adopters like your product or service, they then tell the next group, the early majority. The sweet spot is right there. *You* can't sell directly to the vast group called the early majority, who make up 34 percent of the market—*only the early adopters can.* You will never cross the chasm until the early adopters help you activate it.

Your firm can market to any segment it wants, but in today's transparent, viral world, you cannot sell something on your own; ambassadors or influencers have to sell it for you. Consistently deliver your service so clients can experience it until it becomes their favorite thing; when you build your relationship with your client to that level, you will have earned their trust. If they love you so much, they will tell all their friends and followers about you. When people have an affinity for something, they naturally share that information, and that's the true form of sales—and marketing—today.

Focus on your Three Keys, and your funnel will transform into a megaphone. Your message will come back to you when you do it right and then you can abandon your effort to cast wide nets, hoping for a small close ratio.

How Clients Buy versus Why

A lot of time and money is wasted by professional services firms trying to figure out *why* clients choose to work with the firms that they do. The reasons why clients choose particular firms over others is fairly simple:

- Experience/Expertise: Do you have the specific knowledge that I am willing to pay for?
- Value/Results: Do you have a history of delivering the results I need when I need them?
- Trust: Do I know you? Are you trustworthy? Will you do what you say you will?

So, instead of spending a lot of business development resources trying to influence *why* clients buy, it makes a lot more sense to understand *how* clients buy and then apply the Three Keys. Authors Doug Fletcher and Tom McMakin have provided some significant insights in their book *How Clients Buy.*[4] According to Fletcher and McMakin, clients follow seven steps when buying consulting and professional services:

1. Prospective clients become aware of your existence.
2. They come to understand what you do and how you are unique.
3. They develop an interest in you and your firm.
4. They respect your work and are filled with confidence that you can help.
5. They trust you, confident you will have their best interests at heart.
6. They have the ability to pull the trigger, meaning they are in a position to corral the money and organizational support needed to buy from you.
7. They are ready to do something.

Each prospect must pass through these seven important "gates" before they buy from you and, ultimately, become loyal clients. These cannot be rushed; there is no shortcut. To try to do so is to jeopardize the ultimate success of the sales pursuit.

If you understand your own *why* or *purpose* and then align your sales efforts and messages with *how* clients buy, everything about your sales thinking and process changes. The first three gates are all about telling your firm's story. Your purpose and values are unique to your organization. Use them to make the emotional connection with the buyer. Think of a coffeetable book—you won't open it unless the cover shows something that resonates within you. In order to develop a story that resonates, your team has to see how their pieces align and dissolve the silos. Once you have their attention, your work becomes paramount. But because you live your values with all of your clients, the work is excellent and the buyer can witness how your clients connect differently with your firm. The product of the Three Keys in this process solves the fifth gate. Your prospective client trusts you to solve their problem, instead of simply providing a one-size-fits-all service. At this point, you've done all you can do to influence how the client buys your services. However, the last gates, the money, support, and readiness for the project, will materialize. The alignment, understanding, and connection between your firm and the client ensure project success. And everyone likes to invest in winners.

Learn What Your Clients Need and Solve Their Problem

In professional services, we first think about the client's problem and then how we can solve it. You are looking to deliver a solution to their problem. Whether they seek a single service or four services combined, clients spend money on your solution because they believe fixing their problem has value.

Sometimes when a client calls, they think they are the expert on the specific service they want to buy. For example, they may say, "I need a website to do this and that, so I want you to build a website for me." More often than not, the client actually does not need the services they're requesting, but rather a different set of services. Well-meaning clients tend to identify a symptom as their disease. Your objective is to help clients get to the root of the problem so you can offer the proper solution that cures the disease, not just one symptom.

Your job is to diagnose their problem by asking a lot of questions about what they want to accomplish and why. Knowing their values helps you align your solution with their problem.

Insight Selling versus Solution Selling

Don discusses his view on the current insight-versus-solutions selling debate:

For many years, I considered the idea of solution selling as the most effective approach for professional services. The formula for solution selling was pretty simple: train salespeople to align a solution with an acknowledged customer need and then demonstrate why our solution is better than the competition's. A sales representative begins by identifying customers who recognize a problem that their firm can solve and gives priority to customers who are ready to act. The salesperson asks questions to surface a "hook" that attaches their company's solution to that problem. This sales process may have worked for a poorly informed prospect, but it does not work with the hyper-informed prospect of today.

Customers have radically departed from the old ways of buying. With nearly unlimited information available via the internet, customers are coming to the table armed with a better understanding of their problem and a well-scoped RFP for a solution. Sales leaders increasingly find that their staff is relegated to merely price-driven fulfillment discussions.

To combat this challenge, salespeople must learn to engage potential customers much earlier in the actual sales process, well before customers fully understand their own needs. Do not let the prospect do all the work; help them. Bring insights to the table that are driven by powerful and relevant data and demonstrate your firm's understanding of the issues faced by the prospect. In many ways, this is a strategy as old as sales itself: To win a deal, you've got to get ahead of the RFP.

As stated in a *Forbes* article,[5] "At the end of the day, B2B buyers are looking for a way to prove the value of a potential purchase and build an ironclad business case around it. . . . Insight selling is the most effective means of empowering buyers to succeed in

> gaining organizational buy-in. Only with a deep understanding of a business's needs can sellers provide insights that equip buyers with the wherewithal to build a compelling business case."

Earn Trust with Transparency

You have to set proper expectations with clients and earn trust with them over time. Always keep in mind that trust is built with a client one successful project at a time. When it comes to clients, you should underpromise and overdeliver every time, which means you exceed their expectations. Delivering disappointment and unfulfilled expectations is the quickest way to lose a client's trust.

Transparency about your operations allows them to see how you provide solutions and results. Their trust in you grows when they see how the work gets done. You're also going to have some down days, and clients appreciate transparency and honesty about those times. If you're not willing to give them bad news, ultimately they won't trust you because they'll think you're just blowing smoke at them. You don't want to sugarcoat bad news, but remember, you're solving their problems, not your problems. On those down days, make sure you communicate a solution along with the bad news, so that your client continues to feel trust in how you handle their work.

No Surprises

You want to provide consistent communication to the client about their project. Fran talks about her "No Surprises" rule:

At Advantages, we call challenges "red flags" and "roadblocks." We explain this communication to the client at the beginning of our relationship because we never want to get so far down the line that it is a surprise when the solution doesn't work.

A red flag moment is something that can proactively be fixed, but may cause delays, and the clients should be aware of them. For example, there's a coding problem, or the internet was down. A roadblock is an episode that completely stops a solution from moving forward. For example, when a client doesn't timely provide feedback, the design team cannot move forward.

The end goal is always to stay on time, on budget, and on target. If you've already reached the point of not meeting the end goal and it's the first time the client hears about it, your problem with the client will be greater than the problem itself. For this reason, you need to overcommunicate.

This type of transparency works. When clients are onboarded, we provide upfront communication about timelines and deliverables. This information, along with the regular check-ins, reminds clients that we're working steadily on their behalf behind the scenes while still providing our team sufficient time to get the job done.

As we let the client know all the great progress we're making, I also raise red flags along the way when things aren't going as we thought they would. We ask the client for support and clarification, so the red flags don't become roadblocks. By building trust and communication along the way, we never have to be the bearer of bad news unless something happens completely beyond our control. When that happens, it is our job to pick up the phone and speak to the client. That's always a hard conversation, but it's not about blame, if you align on values, follow your roadblock protocol, and earn your clients' trust. Then, the conversation becomes about determining the path forward to mitigate damage. Clients ultimately respond and respect us for addressing these situations head on, but only after we've established a trust-based relationship.

When the leaders in your firm have strong relationships with your clients and know each other personally, you provide yourself with "client insurance." When there are client problems—and there will be at some point—clients with whom you've built a personal relationship are more likely to give you the opportunity to fix the problem than fire you. Personal connection through your alignment to purpose and values with your clients engenders loyalty and second chances.

There are many ways to build personal relationships with clients that still maintain professional boundaries. Though societal norms and culture may change, respect and common sense are constant and should remain the foundation for any professional relationship.

The "Just Because" Factor

Part of building a personal relationship with your clients is letting them know you think about them even when you aren't working directly on their project. For example, send a card when their child or grandchild graduates from high school or their son gets married. If cards aren't your style, send the client their favorite hard-to-find chocolate or another delicacy they prefer.

Knowing what matters to your client can provide insight into where your values align and the attention to these personal details solidifies your relationship. Show your clients that you truly care about them, not just because they pay your fees, but because they have a meaningful, emotional connection to you.

Through earning trust and understanding with your clients, you'll also collect a loyal tribe of followers. Regardless of which decision-maker buys your services, when they move to, merge with, or start another company they are more likely to hire you because they already trust you and know you're going to deliver excellence.

As mentioned more than once, your objective is to solve the client's problem. Getting to know them personally helps you understand their problem and provide an appropriate solution. However, do not compromise your working relationship. There's a saying, "You can be personable, but you don't have to be personal." There are personal details that make you personable and help build the relationship. However, you need to maintain professional boundaries that will ensure you can still do your job.

Avoid Going Native

"Going native" is a business risk that can occur in professional services firms because consultants often spend time at the client's site. If one of your employees spends five days a week for three years with the client's team, by the third year they are likely to be an integral part of the client's bowling league and attending the bar mitzvahs and baptisms of their client colleagues' children. While those activities are important because they strengthen the relationship, your employees must guard themselves against thinking like they are the client's employees.

As much as employees want to build rapport, there is a distance between your firm and your client that should be maintained. There's a nuance to finding the balance between "close enough" and "too close." Make sure your employees remember who they work for. While they are solving problems and working on behalf of the client, they are also working for the good of your company.

No matter how personal, the relationship should remain a client relationship. By remaining true to your company's values, you will be better equipped to draw the line between relationships and friendships.

The firm bears a strong responsibility for ensuring its consultants don't end up "going native." From professional development to required office days or time away from the client, every firm needs to find ways to build and deepen the connection of its employees to its own shared values and purpose. Your team should align with your clients, but remain connected to your firm. Otherwise, your client will likely lose the value that your firm brought to the project in the first place.

What Can You Do?

Gratify your current clients and attract new ones by doing the following:

- Go deep with your clients in conversations so that you understand not just the service they want, but the problem their company is seeking to address.
- Listen well, and make sure you achieve a full understanding of your client's needs.
- Suggest solutions that will meet the true need of your client, not just their articulated problem.
- Communicate with transparency: underpromise and overdeliver so that you consistently exceed their expectations.
- Build emotional connections with your clients by getting to know them. Spend time with them or send "just because" gifts or cards. However, continue to maintain professional boundaries.
- Attract new clients by communicating your purpose, not your services, in your first conversations.

As your client base and relationships grow, so grows your firm. Soon your firm may need to add many more team members or different types of services to fuel growth. Rather than hire one by one, merging with or acquiring another firm can add to the headcount and services needed to build a larger, more profitable firm. Of course, the firm you want to merge with or acquire must align with your Three Keys: purpose, values, and story. Chapter 8 covers many of the ins and outs of merging with another firm.

Notes

1. https://www.entrepreneur.com/article/278926
2. https://www.sellingpower.com/2014/02/14/10295/do-you-have-a-purpose-or-do-you-just-sell-stuff

3. https://www.ey.com/Publication/vwLUAssets/ey-the-business-case-for-purpose/$FILE/ey-the-business-case-for-purpose.pdf
4. https://sellingsherpa.com/index.php/2018/05/29/how-clients-buy-book-summary/
5. https://www.forbes.com/sites/falonfatemi/2018/08/27/insight-selling-is-the-new-solution-selling/#5f5ebb0b7646

8

Mergers and Acquisitions

"Typically, communication is what makes [a merger] work. The best approach is to just get everyone on one page and communicate the best you can... Once the deal is done you want everyone to feel like they're being treated fairly so that they jump into their job with both feet. If there is uncertainty after the close it can cause real issues in integration."
—Tom Nelson, *"Tom Nelson on Merger Integration Do's and Don'ts"*

Professional services firm mergers and acquisitions play an important part in the strategic landscape of the industry. Combining two different firms allows the new company to reach a larger client audience and offer more comprehensive service solutions. The benefits to both predecessor firms can far outweigh the risks that come with M&A. However, success is not guaranteed; both parties must work incredibly hard to make the transaction and subsequent integration a success.

Don has been intimately involved in close to forty acquisitions and mergers throughout his decades-long career as a CEO of various professional services firms. His accomplished experience, with such transactions and the Three Keys integration, provides the basis for this chapter. Don believes, without doubt, that successful M&A requires the alignment of values between the firms involved in the transaction. This chapter addresses how the Three Keys—purpose, value, and story—impact inorganic growth and demonstrates how values must be in alignment before moving forward with such strategic actions.

Spend Time to Align

Statistics show that between 70 and 90 percent of all professional services mergers and acquisitions fail. A major reason for these failures is the cultural disparity between the organizations. Integrating the cultures of two different companies can be difficult, particularly when the two were competitors before the transaction. Another cause of unsuccessful integrations is the ego of executive leadership. And yet, though these pitfalls are known, few companies exploring a combination take the time to consider how their cultures, including purpose and values, align with one another during the early stages of discussion. According to a recent study,[1] 54 percent of leaders believe that neglecting to audit nonfinancial assets such as organizational culture increases the danger of making the wrong acquisition; however, only 27 percent of them made cultural compatibility a priority during due diligence.

Two firms planning to integrate can only thrive if they prioritize learning about each of the firms' values and then blending these values ahead of anything else. Finding alignment is critical. A relationship that aligns at the brand foundation embodied by the Three Keys will create a more solid footing upon which everything will stand. In their whitepaper, "M&A: Making the Deal Work,"[2] authors Jeff Weirens and Olivier May of Deloitte observe the following:

- Next to your people, your organization's culture is arguably your greatest strategic asset. Your competitors can potentially match your product or service by creating a marketing strategy as equally powerful as yours. But no other organization has your culture. How you do what you do makes you successful.
- When two companies merge, the most apparent cultural differences typically are at the corporate level, where shared beliefs about the company's mission, collective values, and work processes are common foundations of organizational culture.
- While business leaders generally recognize the importance of assessing and managing culture during M&A, many apparently do not feel equipped to make culture-related strategic decisions.

The culture conversation during the M&A process is not a simple "meet and greet." The discussions with an acquisition target or a potential acquirer should be similar to those you have with potential clients (which have been explored at length in Chapter 7). Ask about their purpose, their vision, their values, and the like. Describe how each of the companies would ideally fit together. This is not the time to hold back. Lay your expectations on the table.

Values must emerge in the preliminary discussions. When both parties articulate their values, they can begin to see where overlap exists and where they diverge. Values must be shared up front. If either party can't do that, put the acquisition process on pause. If either of the firms has ever written down their values, this book and the exercises in the appendix can help them to do so. Only with clearly defined values can you truly have the conversation about alignment.

Ultimately, these conversations will establish whether, as leaders, you know each other's companies well enough to determine if you really value the same things and align with the same beliefs. To the financial-minded CFO and corporate strategist, this might sound a little pie-in-the-sky, but the reality is when you align this deeply, every other part of the transaction is made easier.

Connect on Beliefs

Intrinsically, investors want to align with the companies they're acquiring. Just look at the extremely popular reality television series *Shark Tank*. The investors on the show invest in the people with whom they align, not just the companies they present to them. When investors and the visionaries, who lead companies, align on their beliefs, the two parties make an emotional connection that is not easily broken.

As you hold initial discussions with a counterparty, ask questions such as:

- Why is this transaction important to you? What value will it bring to your company—and the world?
- Why do you want to buy our company (or sell yours)? Will it expand your market reach?
- What do you think we can do for you? Can we help you sell new products to your existing clients?
- At the deepest levels, what do you wish to accomplish?
- Do you believe our values and culture have similarities or align?

The questions are not transactional; they are extremely personal. The M&A of professional services companies is all about the people. Take the time to get in sync with the values of the people on the other side of the table. If you fail to do this, you will run into problems down the integration road. Disagreements are typically caused by misaligned values. With proper alignment, however, the next stage of the process is more likely to proceed smoothly.

Embrace the Future Together

Despite mountains of data and executive experiences that clearly show how cultural missteps often derail mergers, many leaders seem more intent on getting a deal done than on getting it done right.

Getting a deal done right means going beyond price, cost synergies, and projected incremental profits.

A successful acquisition means blending what both parties believe in to form a new brand foundation. Though there will be overlap, one company runs on a certain set of values and the other company has a different set of values. This discrepancy provides the perfect opportunity to develop your Three Keys. You need to create an amalgamation of the best purpose, values, and story elements from both companies that will eventually come alive in a new corporate mission and vision. Both companies must have input in developing the new brand foundation to ensure a common rallying point as the new firm evolves.

In addition to comparing values, leaders of potentially merging organizations should compare mission and vision statements. Like values, mission and vision statements indicate where your two companies align—or don't. Likewise, assess the administrative or operational systems and processes to make sure they align with the mission statement, vision, and values. If gaps exist between the mission and values and how they are expressed in the systems and processes, you risk working with a leader who doesn't walk the walk. If this is the case, there may still be reasons to continue with the transaction, but realize that caution should be exercised and know that there will be substantial work to create alignment in the Three Keys.

In their book *Achieving the Execution Edge*, consultants and authors Chris Bart and Elliot Schreiber write, "Meaningful cultural change does not happen quickly. If the attraction still exists for the business move, companies must adjust the execution plan to reflect the extra effort and expenses that will be required to create one cohesive business entity."[3]

CEOs lose sleep thinking about how to successfully scale their professional services organizations. Mergers and acquisitions offer a common and powerful solution to gaining scale. Your firm's culture can either be an obstacle that prevents achieving scale through M&A or a lever that leads to hypergrowth through the acquisition process. When the cultures of two merging companies are extremely different, the leaders must strive to create a new, singular culture and then communicate it consistently. Cultural misalignment on practices such as decision-making and implementation or a clash over strategies will cause inevitable difficulties between individuals at the new firm. When new colleagues begin to work together, if cultural alignment isn't actively pursued, they may frustrate each other by failing to understand or recognize how work should be done.

In an article in the *Harvard Business Review,* Jordana Valencia sums it up quite well: "While hypergrowth companies face many obstacles, research shows that talent is their primary growth challenge. One of their biggest talent priorities is how to scale and maintain culture. Culture, or the underlying beliefs and values that shape an organization, can indeed be difficult to manage when a company scales."[4]

Valencia suggests transferring culture to new employees by training them on expected cultural behaviors. Employees learn by observing others, but abstract values can mean different things to different people. During the post-merger integration of two firms, define and communicate the values of the new culture through behavior that people can observe. Additionally, consider building an accessible digital library of learning content that provides information about knowledge, skills, and attitudes to produce those behaviors.

As we discussed in Chapter 1, culture is driven by leadership. Ensuring the leaders are aligned with values is perhaps never more important than when two once separate entities become one. The leaders, as they embody the values, purpose, and story, will lay the foundation for the culture of the new entity.

Investis Digital

Investis was a twenty-year-old London-based company with a deep heritage in investor relations and corporate communications. ZOG Digital was a fast-growing five-year-old Arizona-based company focused in the area of performance marketing. The two companies wanted to consummate a deal for the purposes of creating a new type of competitor in the market. No one could do what this combined firm could do. It was a very exciting vision. The challenge was to bring together cultures from not only two different firms but also two different countries.

Fortunately, this story is an example of where personal relationships, history, and alignment of values played a big part. The two CEOs had actually known each other for years and even worked together in the past. Their values were in alignment. The high level of trust between the two helped cut through difficult negotiation points, as well as establish an environment of honesty when discussing challenging integration points. Without this trust, there is no question the integration would have been significantly more difficult. Though the executive leadership knew each other, this familiarity did not replace the active exploration for alignment or development of a new set of Three Keys. The entire process was simply made easier.

The Three Keys serve as a guide to create corporate synergy once the acquisition is complete. Establishing a plan to align on the new purpose, values, and story of the emerging organization is critical to prevent becoming one of the statistical failures.

You will want to review the brand foundations of each firm and, quite likely, build new Keys. Starting with purpose, the merged firms can construct new vision and mission statements that articulate the purpose of the newly formed organization.

Bart and Schreiber write, "The new mission is especially pivotal for explaining the new organization to the employees of both companies so that they can all rally around the new mission and get aligned in terms of their behaviors and actions.... Being extremely clear about organizational goals and showing all employees how their work contributes to the new organization's success—especially its mission—are critical to employee engagement."[5]

As the leader of the merger, your job is to connect all the employees of the firm by honestly showing them what will be achieved together, and how it is much greater than what could be achieved separately. It is important to explain why the creation of a new set of values, mission, and vision statements is a better and a more accurate representation of what the firm represents now and in the future.

Create a communication plan to address the impact of changes with all your stakeholders. Allow the evolving purpose and values of your Three Keys guide you. The communication should clearly articulate the "why" behind the reasons for the merger. Describe the strength of the alignment between the firms' values and beliefs. State the objectives for the merger and let the stakeholders know the positive impacts the transaction will have on their relationship with the new firm. Clients are the most important nonemployee stakeholder to address. The leader presents the unified entity to clients. Some clients may say they preferred the original smaller firm—and may even leave. Many other clients will be excited to work with the new firm that will offer them increased capabilities. Every communication related to the merger should remind your employees, your clients, and the leaders of the merging entities about the purpose, values, and story of the new business.

The extent of formal internal and external communication varies during the state of the acquisition process. During the due diligence and the period before signing an MOI or LOI, external communications will likely be limited. Then there will be an official announcement regarding the intent to merge. During the follow-on preclose planning and implementation stage, communication will again dwindle as the close of the transaction approaches. However, on day one of the new entity, the release of another announcement launches the external component of your new third key: the story.

Use the announcement to celebrate the new vision and communicate the integration plans of the new entity. In the months following the close, communication should be released as consistently as milestones are reached. The content of this steady communication should be created to reinforce the values and culture of the new entity.

McKinsey offers an excellent list of best practices on how to create a communications strategy regarding the changes during the entire acquisitions process.[6] We have modified some of these best practices to highlight the opportunities to share the purpose, values, and story of the new organization.

- Focus on business objectives. Energy should be directed to protect and build business value. This is the opportunity to define your purpose and share your story in the market.
- Start early and tailor. Messages should address the stakeholders' evolving needs. If you cannot communicate decisions yet, explain the process.
- Govern tightly. Executives should be directly engaged through clearly defined roles and processes.
- Be conscious of culture. Your culture is a product of your values. Communicate from your values. If, for example, bottom-up thinking is part of the new core values, top-down messaging will not align.
- Be consistent and compelling. This is your story! The more compelling it is, the more successful it will be. All communication should be of high quality and repeatedly reinforced in multiple channels. Communicate five times more than you think you need to.
- Humanize the message. Address what people really care about, in a tone that is responsive to the mood and situation, not overly formal and legalistic. Shared values do not communicate well in legalese.
- Empower your leaders. Actively align leaders, middle managers, and customer-facing staff so that they communicate effectively and consistently. Do not expect the communications function to do all the work.
- Stay up to date. Keep the integration management office and the deal team and major workstreams connected, so that information is up to date and communications are as proactive and effective as possible.
- Be responsive. Collect and respond to feedback regularly and quickly. If you've done the work on Brand-KPIs are discussed later in Chapter 9, you'll be ready to benchmark and course correct from day one.

Be Ready to Compromise

For an acquisition to succeed, the companies involved may need to make compromises to create a new entity. These compromises often involve staff reorganizations and even reductions in force. If both parties have similar organizations, there is a high likelihood of redundant roles. Employees are well aware of these possibilities as talk of a merger heats up. If staff reductions are planned as a result of the transaction, plan to move forward quickly after the signing of the agreements. It is up to the new leaders of the combined firm to authentically use the new values, mission, and vision of the firm to inspire and excite their teams even in the face of possible change.

The firm may also lose employees during acquisitions. The marketplace likely knows the acquisition is planned. The reality of job insecurity may lure good employees to join competitors with a greater perception of stability. However, employees who choose to stay will be the ones who best align with the new blended values and emerging culture.

Decisions on which employees will be left behind, so to speak, are extremely difficult. The purpose and values that the new firm expects to live will be tested and exposed during these challenges. If redundancies are involved, take the time to identify the employees involved who are most enthusiastic about the merger. Share the vision and mission of the combined firm clearly with them. The individuals whose personal values more clearly align with the new organization will likely step forward. Use the Three Keys to create alignment in the new entity, particularly regarding difficult decisions.

After the Close

Even once the merger or acquisition is a go, before the ink dries, there is still work to do that can't be avoided, as Don relays in this story about getting personal in integration planning:

Back in my days at iCrossing, my team was excited by the prospects of closing our first acquisition. We were acquiring a small paid search agency in the San Francisco Bay area. We had worked extremely hard getting this deal to the finish line. This was our first transaction as a team, so our board made us jump through all sorts of hoops to get the approval to move forward. Once we received the approval, we turned our focus to post-close activities.

During our due diligence, we had spoken with the target firm's owner on numerous occasions about how the deal would be communicated to employees. However, the owner was reluctant to tell the employees about the deal until it was imminent. He was concerned that any communication about the deal would cause unnecessary anxiety for the employees surrounding their future at the firm. I fully understood this concern. So, as we approached the closing date, I asked the owner if his employees had been made aware of the impending change of ownership and how they were taking it. I was assured, in his words, that all was good.

The day after closing, I headed to California with iCrossing's founder and my partner, Jeff Herzog, to meet our new employees. The owner met us at the door as we entered the office. All seemed fine. Everyone at the firm was assembled for the first hellos. Then the owner stepped forward and said, "I know I haven't shared any of this with you, but for the past six months, I've had the company up for sale. The good news is we found a buyer that I believe you all will like a lot. They are with us today. Meet Jeff and Don from iCrossing. As a result, today is my last day. It's been a pleasure for the past seven years."

And with that the owner handed me the microphone and walked out the fire exit—not even the front door.

This really happened. Jeff and I looked at each other in total astonishment, but we were not half as astonished as the poor employees. How did this happen, we both thought. Though we

(continued)

would moan about the situation later, and eventually laugh about it, the immediate goal was averting a total disaster. We decided to scrap our carefully prepared presentation about all the great things we were going to do together and started at square one. Jeff spent time explaining the history of iCrossing and how this acquisition fit extremely with our strategy. My job was to quickly get to know the employees and reassure them that we really cared about them and their careers. We spent the rest of that day, and the days to follow, establishing relationships with key employees and giving them the chance to express their concerns.

Long story, short: our first acquisition turned out to be a success, but not without significant anxiety. We overcame the launch-day snafu by overcompensating with personal communications at the individual level. The craziness of how this situation played out with the former CEO demonstrated to me the substantial value in bringing any transaction down to the individual employee level. Regardless of the post-close integration plans you develop, focus directly on the human component (the people, your employees) of the deal to ensure the longer-term success of the transaction.

A Quick Thought on Earn-outs

When mergers happen, redundant roles will be found, up and down the entire org chart. Even executive-level redundancies will have to be addressed. Sometimes the principal of a firm involved may want to exit after the transaction is complete. This turn of events can make the new CEO's role a little bit easier. A new role for someone who effectively was a CEO does not have to be created.

However, sometimes the principal of a firm does not want to leave, or the two firms struggle to reach a financial agreement. If the acquiring firm really wants to purchase the target firm, but does not want to pay the amount the seller wants, or the principal seeks to remain in control, the agreement will often include an earn-out. An earn-out allows the principal at the selling company to remain for a period of time, usually one to three years. If the company reaches certain performance milestones during that time, then the acquirer will make additional payments.

The earn-out style transaction is mentioned merely as a warning, because in many ways, these deals represent the antithesis of successful integration and creation of new shared values. The nature of the transaction encourages the acquirer to leave the selling firm alone until the earn-out period ends. Earn-outs accommodate deals where people have different views on valuation, which often translate into different views on culture, values, and purpose. The accommodation of these differences begs the question of whether an earn-out is appropriate for the purpose-driven organization trying to live according to its Three Keys. Given the extreme challenges of aligning two firms under these conditions, it probably doesn't.

Compromise—or Else

Don shares a story about one of his M&A experiences:

iCrossing was interested in merging with a company named AKQA. (AKQA was, and still is, a quality firm with a deep heritage.) The combination made a lot of sense. iCrossing was a leader in performance marketing, and AKQA was a leader in strategy and design with strong creative talent. Both companies were highly successful in their own right.

Both firms had different private equity groups as primary investors, so when discussions about a merger began, the different primary shareholders wanted their senior executive to run the new company. This would make integration challenging. A resolution had to be reached if the talks were to continue.

The boards of the two firms suggested an idea. Let the two executives meet in Sonoma Valley for a weekend and work out a succession plan. During the weekend the executives hammered

(continued)

out a compromise. AKQA's CEO was ready to step away in the near future, so it was agreed he would carry on as CEO for no more than two years. When the two years were up, iCrossing's CEO would succeed him. The AKQA CEO felt it was important for him to be the CEO during the transition, while I tried to take a longer-term view. This example highlights the potential for a good result when compromise based on personal values—desire for short-term stability or focus on longer-term objectives—can be reached during M&A discussions.

Sadly, the deal ultimately fell apart for other reasons. Even though the deal didn't work out, we had the opportunity to discuss and find alignment on what was important to them, though that term probably wasn't used back then to describe what happened. If the deal had gone through, the digital landscape would have changed significantly. Hindsight is always 20/20.

What Can You Do?

Despite the odds, successful M&A is possible. It will take time and patience—inorganic growth is hard work but the result can be well worth it.

Mergers and acquisitions are your opportunity not only to create a new entity, but to get your employees inspired and enthusiastic about being part of an exciting new company. Before you get started, you'll want to remember a few important things:

- Both parties should take the time up front to understand each other's values and look for the alignment. This cannot be emphasized enough. Your beliefs and values must be aligned enough to survive disagreements and rough spots. Write down your values, and then trade lists so you can see where you're both already on the same page.

- Don't forget to get to know one another. This is an important relationship to build, so ask questions that reveal the authentic person behind the corporate leader.
- It can be easy to get caught up in the idea of profit while making the deal, but think about your purpose and values. What is the change in the world you want to make by working together with the new firm?
- To paraphrase Kenny Rogers, know when to compromise—and when to walk away. Making deals can be intoxicating, but "deal fever" can lead to bad transactions. When you clearly articulate your firm's purpose and values, you won't be blinded by the romance of the deal itself. Prepare ahead of time by writing down your bottom line that holds to your values and refer to it when the discussion warrants it.
- Integration is about sweating the details. Go through each layer of the organization. When you've got two people in the same role, think about where people can go and where you have to make cuts, but apply your Three Keys liberally during challenging situations.
- Don't forget to get excited! Be sure to let both parties know what's happening so people aren't in the dark. And then answer questions, highlight the benefits (in writing, so your new team has something to refer back to), and celebrate the future you're all building together.

Deals are a legacy of the leader, and whether they fail or succeed often rests on their shoulders. Consistent success takes experience, and the more deals you do, the better you get at it. Now that you've closed that deal, integrated the two firms, and are now living the shared values and purpose of the new company, what could possibly be left to do? Measure your success.

In an article for *OD Practitioner*,[7] "Driving Culture Transformation During Large-Scale Change," Wendy L. Heckelman, Sheryl Unger, and Christina Garofano propose that measurement and reporting of progress and success are critical components to ensure ongoing success. Measurement provides leaders and change champions with needed feedback on gaps between existing and desired behavior and beliefs, which enables focus on areas with the biggest impact on performance and results. Measuring organizational culture is critical. In the next chapter, we discuss measuring your culture and the impact it has on the success of your organization.

Notes

1. https://www2.deloitte.com/content/dam/Deloitte/us/Documents/mergers-acqisitions/us-ma-making-the-deal-work-compendium.pdf
2. Ibid.
3. https://www.canadianmetalworking.com/article/management/mergers-and-acquisitions-growth-strategy-or-minefieldr-
4. https://hbr.org/2019/06/scaling-culture-in-fast-growing-companies
5. http://businessfocusstlucia.com/painful-marriages-mergers-miscarry-board-can-make-work/
6. https://www.mckinsey.com/business-functions/organization/our-insights/communications-in-mergers-the-glue-that-holds-everything-together
7. https://cdn.ymaws.com/www.odnetwork.org/resource/resmgr/odp45_3/vol45no3-heckelman_et_al.pdf

9

Measure
Your Purpose

If you can't measure it, you can't improve it.
—Peter Drucker, management consultant, educator,
and author

Throughout the book, we have talked about injecting the Three Keys into every aspect of a business to create alignment with all stakeholders. When alignment is intentionally developed, momentum is created inside the business, and teams go further, faster. When employees are happier and more fulfilled, they are dramatically more productive. The result has been alluded to in each chapter: greater profitability. This can be represented by a simple equation:

$$\text{DIRECT STAKEHOLDER ALIGNMENT} = \text{INCREASED PROFITABILITY}$$

But how can a leader determine if their business is truly living its purpose, values, and story? While the bottom line serves as an implicit indicator of business health, there are too many variables (market forces, economic trends, sales systems, etc.) and it is too difficult to determine the impact the Three Keys, and specifically purpose, have on profits by just that metric alone.

In the HBR survey cited earlier in the book, executives stated, "Companies need to do a better job embedding their purpose in the organization, particularly in leadership development and training, in employee performance metrics and rewards, and in operations." Further on, Michael Beer is quoted as saying that purpose "has to be driven, operationally and in depth, by the CEO and top leadership team. That takes a lot of skill and understanding to do well, which is why so few companies really can pull it off." And Marc Ventresca said, "Businesses are just beginning to understand how to integrate and measure performance tied to purpose."[1]

If you are not determined to measure something, it is impossible to manage it efficiently or effectively. The world's best companies are not the best by luck; they are consistently measuring their sales, churn, overhead, and so on. But those metrics only provide insight into one side of the equation: profitability. In order to achieve clarity into the stakeholder alignment side, to determine whether a company is authentically living and articulating its purpose, leaders need to assess how well their purpose is infused into every part of the business. Measuring purpose has a direct correlation to increasing sales, decreasing churn, and achieving more efficient overhead. Another simple equation:

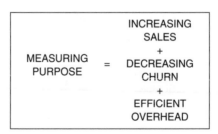

$$\text{MEASURING PURPOSE} = \frac{\text{INCREASING SALES}}{+} \frac{\text{DECREASING CHURN}}{+} \text{EFFICIENT OVERHEAD}$$

Now, let's combine the two equations:

$$
\begin{array}{l}
\text{DIRECT} \\
\text{STAKEHOLDER} \\
\text{ALIGNMENT} \\
+ \\
\text{MEASURING} \\
\text{PURPOSE}
\end{array}
=
\begin{array}{l}
\text{INCREASED} \\
\text{PROFITABILITY} \\
\text{(INCREASING SALES} \\
\text{+ DECREASING CHURN} \\
\text{+ EFFICIENT OVERHEAD)}
\end{array}
$$

Fran and her leadership team at Advantages developed a dashboard to institutionalize the above equation into businesses all over the world. The dashboard measures brand-focused *Key Purpose Indicators*. Professional services firms conventionally track and measure operationally focused Key Performance Indicators (KPIs), but it's time they do the same for brand-focused Key Purpose Indicators. The easiest way to articulate the difference between the two KPIs is: Brand-KPIs versus Operational-KPIs. To become the most efficient, effective, and profitable professional services company possible, you need to track both forms.

Who Owns the Key Purpose Indicators?

Performance measurement specialist Stacey Barr writes, "The most appropriate person to be the performance owner of a particular measure is the person who is responsible for managing the process, function, or activity that the measure is monitoring."[2]

When you begin measuring Key *Purpose* Indicators linked to culture, mission, vision, and values, as the leader of the company you must take responsibility and own those KPIs. You have the intimate knowledge and deep connection with the company you lead, the values driving its performance, and the culture sustaining its growth. Others may help monitor and interpret the KPI reporting, but ultimately you are responsible for defining the measurement and overseeing the monitoring, as well as interpreting feedback, trends, and communicating performance results in order to execute more actionable strategies and informed decisions.

In this chapter, we explore how to measure purpose in four steps:

1. Determine what to measure.
2. Determine how it should be measured.
3. Collect the right data.
4. Analyze the data correctly.

What to Measure?

Once a solid brand foundation has been developed (your purpose, values, and story), ask yourself: *What are the things inside this company that indicate we are definitively living our purpose?* Those answers become your Key *Purpose* Indicators.

Brand-focused KPIs work much the same way as standard operationally focused KPIs surrounding financials, sales goals, or product development. For instance, within the sales team, it's a best practice to track how many prospects they called, how many conversations they had, and how many meetings they set up during the week. Then, as in any sales funnel, you want to know from the number of meetings how many converted into proposals, then how many proposals converted into real jobs. Throughout the process, the sales team tracks their way through the funnel and measures progress every step of the way. At the end of the week, you are able to view the metrics and understand exactly how efficient the sales team is because every step is concretely measured. Those measurements provide critical insights to measure where the sales team may be missing the mark, if changes need to be made, or if they should accelerate more of what they are already doing.

Sales processes seem simpler to measure than an intangible asset like purpose, but that does not detract from the absolute necessity to measure it. When businesses consistently measure purpose, they become attuned to the strength of their purpose and its growth, which directly translates into notable shifts in culture, communication, collaboration—and profit.

Implementing a dedicated Key Purpose Indicators dashboard alongside a traditional operationally focused KPI dashboard creates a 360-degree feedback loop to accelerate your momentum. Developing measurements for purpose is an agile, iterative process that matures over time as you become more comfortable and familiar with the tool. This dashboard is not for measuring against what other firms do; it is for measuring your present business purposefulness against its past. With that in mind, do not expect to nail the right metrics and feedback loops right out of the gate. Business can be messy at times, and getting this aligned strategically for the long term is no different.

Purpose should be viewed as a strategic asset that has holistic implications for the business so it is vitally important to properly measure it. Therefore, it is necessary to break down purpose into areas, divisions, and components within the business where it can be best measured. This holds for both internal and external aspects of the business, from customer relations to vendors, to market trends and employee wellness. The potential markers are endless. So determine the 8 to 10 markers that, based on your experience, matter the most as linchpins for the future viability of your solid brand foundation.

How Do We Measure These Things?

Key Purpose Indicators are measured both organically and through prompted feedback.

- **Organic data includes:** unsolicited comments, press-related discussions, references to the company, informal feedback and suggestions from employees and vendors. Organic data is collected year-round 24/7, not on a time schedule or fiscal year. In order to properly collect organic data for a Key Purpose Indicators analysis, you must attune your ears to what is going on in, around, and throughout the company, and train your team to do the same.

Contextual awareness is a skill that is developed, practiced, and honed. Are the things employees say "echoing" the purposeful words you use when referencing the vision and values of the business? Can the compliments and criticisms you receive be categorized as fulfilling or disregarding a particular value? This is the type of data that needs to be captured. Yes, that is hard to do because organic data is unpredictable. So, there needs to be a reliable and predictable system for capturing it. Identify a centralized location where it is easy for the entire company enter organic feedback, maybe in a recreation room. This will allow for the data to continue to flow and periodically generate patterns of insights and trends within the sentiment of the company culture. On the other hand, this can also be as simple as opening a shared document with prompts for the date, who submitted the feedback, and their honest perspectives.

- <u>Prompted feedback includes:</u> more formal and regular survey requests. These include things such as client surveys and quarterly employee review sessions. Most companies have already implemented some form of these data collection methods. However, they have not yet added the purpose-oriented prompts that are integral to generating a holistic view of any business.

Internal Measurement

Internal measurements of brand-focused KPIs measure purpose in culture for employees and outside stakeholders. Employees are the most obvious indicator of whether the business is living its purpose. But at a more granular level, it is critical to take the pulse of employees as both individuals and groups through open and unprompted communication as well as on scheduled intervals. Employee satisfaction should be measured on a monthly or quarterly basis with face-to-face meetings and surveys. The questions asked should include culture-driven and values-oriented questions related to the specific purpose of the business, as well as perspectives on the effectiveness of overall internal communication, wellness, environment, and support.

Culture, Purpose, and Performance

Most leaders agree on which measurable elements create a good business and a measurable bottom line: efficiency, productivity, innovation, employee retention, and the like. But there is a big missing piece to this equation, especially in professional services-based businesses: How does a leader qualitatively and quantitatively measure culture?

There has been a mountain of research in recent years, tying the elements of culture back to financial performance. Culture is the qualitative method for achieving a leader's long-term commitment to delivering excellence—excellent service to customers, excellent returns for stakeholders, and an excellent environment for employees—guided by a clearly articulated, vivid vision.

A culture anchored in shared values, driven by purpose, and communicated to employees and clients through your story supports and encourages efficiency, productivity, innovation, and retention. These measurable objectives are the byproduct of culture, essentially the foundation of a company's success.

Culture has increasingly become a marketing differentiator because it directly correlates to well-developed brand foundation. Think of capturing emerging competitive advantage this way:

- The stronger a culture, the stronger a competitive weapon it becomes.
- The stronger the weapon, the stronger the brand advantage created.
- The stronger the brand advantage, the deeper the marketing engagement developed.
- The deeper the engagement, the stronger the competitive differentiation.
- Repeat.

The hardest challenge to overcome when developing Key Purpose Indicators is the fact that when you start, there isn't any data to measure your performance against. As a leader begins to build Brand-KPIs, they are establishing fundamental baselines for the business. However, as the process begins, it is also important to learn how purpose-driven every team across the business believes they currently are.

An excellent strategy for discovering how well the company is living its purpose is asking employees to compare the firm culture with that of cultures from their previous employers. An even further step would be to inquire about the workplaces of their friends and family. Whether it is you or one of your senior managers, make sure to directly ask if the company can live its purpose in a better, larger, and more holistic set of ways. In face-to-face meetings, ask employees questions that organically reveal how well they know and connect to the company's purpose and values. Include prompts such as: "Can you think of one way that we truly live one of our values and one way that we could do a better job?"

See Figures 9.1 and 9.2 for examples from Fran's work across the world.

External Measurements

External measurements of brand-focused KPIs correspond to how stakeholders outside the business feel about how well the company delivers on its purpose. The most obvious aspect to measure is customer satisfaction, but external measurement also includes vendor relationships, industry reputation, and market perception.

Key Purpose Indicator
Employee Culture Feedback Survey

Our Shared Values

1. Live Up to Our Promise
2. Deliver on Time
3. Go the Extra Mile
4. Communicate the Process
5. Be Prepared for the Unexpected

Our Why To provide clarity so that everyone has the power to make the best choices.

Our Vision A world where everyone has the ability to make the most informed choices.

Our Mission To provide information and clarity to anyone anywhere looking to ship internationally.

KEY: 1 = Negative \ 10 = Positive

1. Do you feel physically and psychologically safe in the workplace? 1 2 3 4 5 6 7 8 9 10 N/A

2. How comfortable are you with approaching leaders with issues/problems/mistakes? 1 2 3 4 5 6 7 8 9 10 N/A

3. How well do you feel your opinion is valued? 1 2 3 4 5 6 7 8 9 10 N/A

4. How well does leadership and the company in general fulfill its promises to you? 1 2 3 4 5 6 7 8 9 10 N/A

5. Are responses and feedback given timely? 1 2 3 4 5 6 7 8 9 10 N/A

6. Do you feel like leadership will do whatever it takes to keep you happy, challenged, and growing? 1 2 3 4 5 6 7 8 9 10 N/A

7. Do you have a clear understanding of what is expected day to day and project to project? 1 2 3 4 5 6 7 8 9 10 N/A

8. Which value do you feel we fulfill best? _____

9. Which value do you believe needs the most improvement? _____

Figure 9.1   KPI Dashboard Employee Culture Feedback Survey.

Key Purpose Indicator
Employee Culture Dashboard

Objective:

Our objective is to measure how well we are living our Purpose, and particularly our values, internally. We ask general culture questions, and several values-oriented questions.

Procedure:

Every quarter we require our employees to submit anonymous surveys in response to the type of questions mentioned above, using the 1 (worst) to 10 (best) scale.

The result for each question is calculated by adding all scores and dividing by the number of surveys received and then visually presenting the total as a percentage of the aggregate score in chart form. All scores are then combined to give an overall result. If there is a significantly low area, companywide meetings are held to take input on how to correct.

Results:

Results are plotted on bar charts so that we can visually see changes that occur throughout the year.

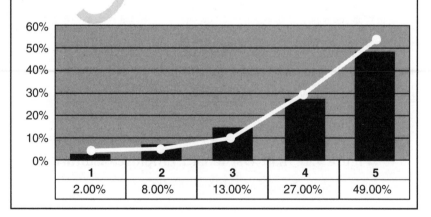

1	2	3	4	5
2.00%	8.00%	13.00%	27.00%	49.00%

Figure 9.2   KPI Employee Culture Dashboard.

Hiring Meets Purpose to Elevate Performance

We often hear great leaders explain the importance of people inside their organizations. Hiring great people is fundamental to any organization's long-term success. As Lawrence Bossidy, former COO of General Electric and CEO of Allied Signal, said, "Nothing we do is more important than hiring and developing people. At the end of the day, you bet on people, not on strategies."

How you develop your employees is where any long-term competitive advantage lives. Talent determines whether your professional services company will thrive, survive, or wither away in the future. As leaders, we do not often see reality from this perspective, but the truth is that employees are responsible for manifesting the values of the company. Yet very often, there is minimal measurement of how employees are living the company's purpose and the link to the human resources function in the business. At the end of the quarter, when measuring sales, revenues, and profits, leaders often forget that the most important indicator for long-term company viability and success is a high-quality hiring strategy.

As soon as you begin taking your brand foundation seriously, the future of your company's success is based on the new strategies underlying the hiring process. As discussed earlier, when employees are hired based first on cultural fit and aligned values, the outcomes will speak for themselves: happier, more engaged employees, greater retention, increased efficiency. In cooperation with your Brand-KPIs, implementing an annual scorecard process to measure the success of the hiring process is a straightforward strategy for a better human resources function.

Client Satisfaction from Purpose Drives Performance

In an article on the development of a mission statement linking customer mission to a wider social mission, Gideon Rosenblatt writes, "Companies cannot create real customer success without customers, because success depends upon how successful customers use their services to achieve their own objectives. This sounds obvious, but clarity on this point will deepen one's understanding of the customer mission."[3]

Maximizing client satisfaction is one of the strongest metrics for maximizing profitability, although other factors such as cost control, productivity, and operational strategy also impact the bottom line. The best practice to understand is to know which services clients enjoy the most, and why. In addition to meeting with clients in person, as described earlier, there are more in-depth tactics for uncovering further information about clients, including surveys, data collection, and the powerful brand-focused Key Purpose Indicator dashboard.

Customer Satisfaction

Begin by issuing monthly or quarterly customer satisfaction surveys to clients, as well as upon completion of each project. The simplest way is to use the standard 1-to-10 ranking system. Systems that use a 1-to-5 rank simply do not leave enough room for nuance and improvement.

Keep surveys short and easy to fill out. This will dramatically increase compliance with survey requests. In the beginning, do not get discouraged by low response rates. Seek to continue shortening the survey and let clients know how important the information they provide is to your company. If you clearly articulate this to clients, their sense of obligation to comply will increase.

Start with general questions, such as "How would you rank our services?" Then drill down into more specific purpose-related questions. For each of your values, have at least one question to test whether clients feel you are totally fulfilling that value promise. We recommend having the company values written on the survey, so clients have an easier time determining to what extent those values have been lived. Flag all incoming comments related to particular employees or parts of the process so that you can analyze them during employee performance reviews and monthly or quarterly organization-wide reviews.

Always have one open-ended question, such as "Was there an interaction (positive or negative) that stood out in your mind as something encapsulating your overall experience with our company?" (See Figure 9.3. for an example.) Although these types of answers cannot be quantitatively calculated for Brand-KPIs, they provide deeper insight into the kinds of positive and negative feedback the business has received. Such statements also provide necessary context to employees about the numeric results received from clients.

All the data from each feedback cycle should be compiled, organized, and, ideally, presented graphically to senior leadership. This provides a Brand-KPI "audit," and will further institutionalize the importance of the Key Purpose Indicator dashboard as a strategic metric for the viability of the business.

Client Retention and Referrals

Another way to measure whether purposeful connection is occurring during client interactions is the retention level of existing clients and the number of new clients they refer. On a fundamental level, tracking customer retention should already be a metric that leadership focuses on, but in order to test your business's purpose, ask referring clients why they referred someone to you. Pay careful attention to their response to hear if the language they use directly reflects the stated purpose and values of the business. It is a well-known best practice of

Key Purpose Indicator
Client/Customer Feedback Survey

Our Shared Values

1. Live Up to Our Promise
2. Deliver on Time
3. Go the Extra Mile
4. Communicate the Process
5. Be Prepared for the Unexpected

Our Why To provide clarity so that everyone has the power to make the best choices.

Our Vision A world where everyone has the ability to make the most informed choices.

Our Mission To provide information and clarity to anyone anywhere looking to ship internationally.

KEY: 1 = Negative \ 10 = Positive

1. How well did we deliver on what we promised?   1 2 3 4 5 6 7 8 9 10

2. How well did we keep to our deadlines?   1 2 3 4 5 6 7 8 9 10

3. Did we do whatever extra was required?   1 2 3 4 5 6 7 8 9 10

4. How well were you kept apprised of the process?   1 2 3 4 5 6 7 8 9 10

5. How well did we handle unexpected changes?   1 2 3 4 5 6 7 8 9 10

6. In looking at our values to the right, how well did we live up to those values?   1 2 3 4 5 6 7 8 9 10

7. When looking at our values above, is there a particular instance that you feel showed that we truly lived one of those values or failed to live one of those values? If so, please let us know. _____

_____

8. How likely are you to recommend us to others?   1 2 3 4 5 6 7 8 9 10

Figure 9.3   KPI Client/Customer Feedback Survey.

business that keeping an existing customer is significantly more cost-effective than developing a new one. To grow, every business needs to do both effectively. But if the business is not retaining customers, then something is deeply flawed somewhere. Your goal is to create and cultivate a certain type of client, and the Brand–KPI dashboard leads the way, with its corresponding process to uncover valuable feedback.

The types of clients you want are "sticky." Cultivating "sticky" clients does not mean they need you all the time; as discussed in Chapter 7, you do not want them attached by an umbilical cord. Instead, focus on delivering results based on both your Brand-KPI and Operational-KPI dashboards, and the level of retained and recurring business will increase. The challenge lies in balancing the intensity of work to deliver results. That means planning out two things: enough time to generate the results, and concrete methods to measure those results. Since the project for each client will be different and so will interactions with them, it is important to start at square one.

When first measuring purpose-based client feedback, the goal is first and foremost to create a baseline for measurement. After the first few quarters of implementing the Brand-KPI Dashboard, the ability to set tangible growth goals with strong measurements against previous quarters becomes increasingly easier and more transparent. Most importantly, the areas where the business needs the most improvement with emerge organically. (See Figure 9.4.) As those improvement areas become clear, it will be increasingly easier to determine whether certain measuring tools require tweaking.

Vendor/Supplier Alignment

This is often the most overlooked yet most impactful measurement for how deeply nested purpose has become inside your company. When vendors and suppliers can succinctly state your purpose and values back to you, you know that you are living your purpose and attracting like-minded individuals and clients. (See Figures 9.5 and 9.6.)

Send your major vendors and suppliers surveys similar to those sent to clients, but directed to the vendor relationship. Sure, vendors have a vested interest in complimenting you, but there are always areas of improvement to discover. Additionally, doing so provides an opportunity to coach vendors on how to describe and discuss your business to others—a megaphone in the making!

Key Purpose Indicator
Customer Satisfaction Dashboard

Objective:

Our objective is to show an improvement in purpose-based customer satisfaction, particularly aligned to values. In the first round or two, we are setting a baseline score against which we measure moving forward in order to gauge whether we are improving in the way we live our values. We ask one question that relates to each shared value as well as a general values-oriented open-ended question. We include our values on the survey for ease of reference.

Procedure:

Every month/quarter and at the completion of every large phase, we ask our customers of completed contracts to rate the above categories from 1 (worst) to 10 (best). Completed feedback forms are circulated to the appropriate managers so that good feedback is recognized by senior management and any negative comments or low marks can be addressed.

The result for each question is calculated by adding all scores and dividing by the number of surveys received and then visually presenting the total as a percentage of the aggregate score in chart form. All scores are then combined to give an overall result.

Results:

Results are plotted on bar charts so that we can visually see changes that occur throughout the year.

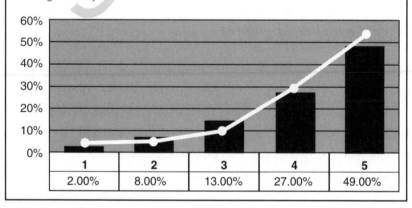

1	2	3	4	5
2.00%	8.00%	13.00%	27.00%	49.00%

Figure 9.4   KPI Customer Satisfaction Dashboard.

Key Purpose Indicator
Partner/Vendor Feedback Survey

Our Shared Values

1. Live Up to Our Promise
2. Deliver on Time
3. Go the Extra Mile
4. Communicate the Process
5. Be Prepared for the Unexpected

Our Why To provide clarity so that everyone has the power to make the best choices.

Our Vision A world where everyone has the ability to make the most informed choices.

Our Mission To provide information and clarity to anyone anywhere looking to ship internationally.

KEY: 1 = Negative \ 10 = Positive

1. Did we provide what you asked for, including proper payment?   1 2 3 4 5 6 7 8 9 10

2. How well did we keep to deadlines?   1 2 3 4 5 6 7 8 9 10

3. Did we do whatever extra was required?   1 2 3 4 5 6 7 8 9 10

4. When you needed us, how easy was it to get to the person you needed?   1 2 3 4 5 6 7 8 9 10

5. How well were you kept apprised of the process?   1 2 3 4 5 6 7 8 9 10

6. How well did we handle unexpected changes?   1 2 3 4 5 6 7 8 9 10

7. How well did we live up our values?   1 2 3 4 5 6 7 8 9 10

8. How likely are you to recommend us to others?   1 2 3 4 5 6 7 8 9 10

9. When looking at our values above, is there a particular instance that you feel showed that we truly lived one of these values or failed to live one of these values? _____

_____

_____

Figure 9.5   KPI Partner/Vendor Feedback Survey.

Key Purpose Indicator
Key Partner Dashboard

Objective:
Our objective is to show an improvement in understanding of our Purpose by our Key Partners/Vendors and determine whether we are living our values throughout our external relationships. In the first round or two, we are setting a baseline score against which we measure moving forward in order to gauge whether we are improving in the way we live our values with our Key Partners. We ask one question that relates to each shared value as well as a general values-oriented open-ended question. We include our values on the survey for ease of reference.

Procedure:
Every quarter and at the completion of every large phase, we ask our Partner/Vendors to rate the above categories from 1 (worst) to 10 (best).

The result for each question is calculated by adding all scores and dividing by the number of surveys received and then visually presenting the total as a percentage of the aggregate score in chart form. All scores are then combined to give an overall result.

Results:
Results are plotted on bar charts so that we can visually see changes that occur throughout the year.

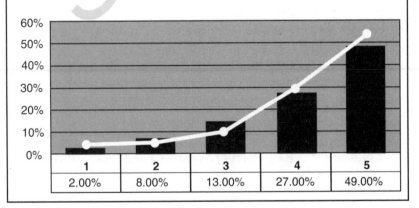

	1	2	3	4	5
	2.00%	8.00%	13.00%	27.00%	49.00%

Figure 9.6   KPI Key Partner Dashboard.

Measurement and Performance

From the very beginning, it is imperative to define specific goals to measure with both the Brand-KPI Dashboard and the Operational-KPI Dashboard. Most leaders are familiar with SMART goals: Specific, Measurable, Attainable, Relevant, and Time-bound. Try to have every KPI, whether brand or operational, meet the SMART definition. Doing so will provide clear data to determine whether the goal is met and where improvement is needed.

Review and update each set of KPIs quarterly. After the baseline has been established, begin to measure progress against prior quarters and years. Key Purpose Indicators and the dashboard are not focused on competing against others in your space. Instead, you are measuring yourself against yourself, with a simple question in mind: "How much more purposeful can we become?" There will always be opportunities for improvement. However, if you intentionally seek 1 percent improvement in alignment with your Three Keys across every aspect of the business, increased success and profitability are inevitable. Using both KPI dashboards provides insights needed to measure current performance against past performance, both internally and externally.

Remember, the whole goal with a brand-driven, purpose dashboard is to build a bridge to broaden and deepen the insights gathered. This enables a leader to develop more actionable insights, which translate into new, differentiated strategies. This is where the crux of a differentiated relationship with employees, clients, and all stakeholders lives.

What Can You Do?

This should be blatantly apparent by now: values and purpose must be aligned across every aspect of the business. There is a lot of information to collect to measure the impact of those values, so to begin developing an action plan start with the following:

- Write out Key Purpose Indicator goals and post them where you and your team are forced to view them on a daily basis. Doing so makes sure the goals of the business are clear and drives alignment of every decision through purpose-driven goals.
- Track progression toward goals by creating a purpose-based scoreboard. This is how anyone in the company can view how the team is collectively measuring up against the goals of the business, as well as those of competitors. If the business is just starting, compare progress from week to week or month to month to show an onward and upward trend of improvement.
- Acknowledge team productivity and ways they contribute to the exhibition of the business's purpose. Affirm their accomplishment in writing—and maybe include a treat, too! Remember: profit is not possible without direct participation by engaged employees.

Notes

1. https://www.ey.com/Publication/vwLUAssets/ey-the-business-case-for-purpose/$FILE/ey-the-business-case-for-purpose.pdf
2. https://www.staceybarr.com/measure-up/what-does-a-kpi-owner-do/
3. https://www.the-vital-edge.com/mission-statement-h/

Conclusion: Use the Three Keys

This book is not for professional services firms that want to rest on the laurels of their past successes. We wrote this book for leaders who are driven to achieve incredible results through values-based leadership. Purpose-led firms learn and live their Three Keys to achieve enduring success.

Human beings are hardwired for group cooperation and shared values. Your firm is a group of humans who collaborate to create a service that is sold for the benefit of other humans. The Three Keys leverage the human desire for shared values. Shared values provide the channel for your story to strategically flow forward to achieve its mission. Shared values create an essence—a visceral feeling—which becomes a path to develop stories, which trigger emotional connections. Apple provides an illustrative example.

Apple's product line differentiation has been based on challenging the status quo and urging the world to "think different." Their customers buy the Apple story as much as they purchase their products. Apple's shared values inform everything they produce. Their products are beautiful, simple to operate, and extremely user-friendly—these are shared values at Apple. This example is a simple distillation of the

Three Keys in action. Throughout this book we have applied this thinking to the management of professional services firms.

The Three Keys create the brand foundation that guides how you communicate everything your company does and strategically drives all aspects of the business. With the Three Keys, the physical and aesthetic elements of a business combine with the verbal and emotional elements to create a full-circle experience for every stakeholder interaction. Repeatable. Scalable. Differentiated. Strategic. Holistic. Profitable.

We have presented this concept with the following equation:

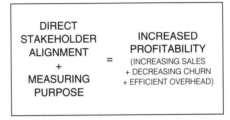

Simply stated, this formula describes the success achieved with the emotional connection created between you, your stakeholders, and the broader market using the Three Keys.

The Three Keys become tangible assets when they are intentionally applied to a brand foundation supporting the myriad integrated touchpoints where your firm shows up in the world. From your logo to your online and print presence, from a tradeshow booth to a bus-stop kiosk, or even on the social media feed of an influencer, your Three Keys form the foundation.

Strategic leadership of 21st-century professional services companies requires starting with a purposeful brand foundation, which is then institutionalized through a culture, led explicitly by shared values. When human beings share the same set of beliefs working toward achieving a vision grander than themselves, explicit and implicit connections happen, and alignment quickly follows. This translates into a more rewarding, productive, and profitable workplace environment, fueled by passion, that inevitably produces a greater focus on performance, leading to enhanced results. Better results lead to further institutionalizing beliefs, which then direct culture toward further alignment.

Purpose is real. It has a tangible, practical, verifiable impact on the financial future of your company. Employees who find meaning in their work become an inspiration to others around them. Their attitude and commitment to the company become infectious. These aligned employees become the culture ambassadors who set the tone for everyone else within the company. These are the types of employees who defy conventional economic assumptions about self-interest, and who understand the power of community. Your goal is to nurture, identify, and empower as many of these employees as possible. Their focus, energy, and commitment will move organizational transformation mountains at lightning speed.

Purposeful leaders must anchor themselves steadfastly in their values. When you are unwavering in your beliefs, you hire, fire, team-build, and design your organizational structure around those beliefs. Through your story, you will attract the right clients and avoid attracting the wrong ones. You can deepen your relationships with all of your stakeholders based on how you deliver on your values.

You, as the leader, must clearly communicate your vision for the firm and the values that will guide you to accomplish that vision. The Three Keys will always be the place where any strategic journey for your company begins. A clear message and story unify your team, which creates momentum toward your vision, and a future-forward perspective every single stakeholder can emotionally connect with.

This book is a guide for how to lead a values-based professional services firm. Put the tools into action. Define your purpose, your values, and your story. Take the time to think deeply about the ideas discussed in this book. If you are dedicated to achieving your dreams, the Three Keys are an invaluable tool to get there. When professional services leaders become clear on their purpose, values, and story, their firms go further faster. Now, go get started.

Appendix:
The Three Keys
to a Purposeful
Brand Foundation

You have read extensively how the Three Keys—purpose, value, and story—are interwoven into and directly impact every facet of a business. But how does a leader begin to take intentional action to identify and define their company purpose, values, and story?

Most companies choose to retain outside expert advice to develop and strategically implement their brand foundation. Whether a small startup or a Fortune 50 company, this is pretty much a best practice. It is exceedingly difficult to honestly see and evaluate all of the aspects of individual and business purpose, values, and stories.

However, if you possess the courage to develop each of the keys yourself, this appendix is chock full of the help you will need, inspired by the comprehensive frameworks Advantages executes for its clients. The answers you require to develop your rock-solid brand foundation are all out there, but be warned: to uncover them will take a hefty investment of elbow grease and time.

To recap, a purpose-driven brand is built from the bottom up, and like any enduring structure, there must first be a rock-solid foundation. A brand foundation is a set of written materials that are authentic, intentional, and customized—no cookie-cutter approach here. These materials directly reflect the character and community of your company, and become the starting point for any and all communications.

Let's quickly review the Three Keys:

- **Key #1: Purpose.** A business's purpose is composed of three elements:
  - Why: your cause, belief, reason for being
  - Vision: the impact you want to achieve in the world
  - Mission: the rallying cry you are committed to executing on every single day, seeking to move the needle closer to achieving your vision
- **Key #2: Values.** These are the unchanging moral and ethical imperatives that implicitly and explicitly drive the overall behavior of your organization, both internally and externally. There are two sets of values, core values and shared values:
  - Core values are individual values derived from your own personal strengths.
  - Shared values are business-wide values derived from the core values of the leadership team.
- **Key #3: Story.** A business's story comprises the strategic arrangement of its purpose and values in a way that evokes a visceral connection with anyone who experiences it.

Now, let's dig into the details!

Find Powerful Purpose

The first step in building a solid brand foundation is to discover your true purpose. There are three steps to the process, beginning with identifying why you do what you do.

Step 1: Entering the Why Mindset

The first step in finding your Why is to identify exactly what in the world inspires you. We are talking about what inspires you deep down as an individual, at the core of your soul—not what you want, as a businessperson, leader, or entrepreneur. (Don't worry, we will get to that.)

To get started, let's undertake a simple exercise. Grab a pen and paper. Then write down at least 28 things that deeply inspire and motivate you to jump out of bed every single morning.

When we facilitate this exercise with clients, they usually begin at the surface level, with the daily stuff they have to do (brush their teeth, get the kids to school, walk the dog, etc.). All of this is important for sure, but none of these tasks are exhilarating. Therefore, none of them are the target of this exercise. As clients continue to write and move further down the list, answers become deeper, more distinctly personal, and ultimately more purposeful. We are asking you to go to a deep place within yourself. If you cannot get there on the first try, it might be better to take a walk, have a stretch, meditate, or grab a bite to eat. You need to be in a centered, reflective position to dig this deep. No excuses!

When your page starts to fill up and it gets harder to write down answers, you are finally getting past the surface and wading into the essential aspects of your true being. The top indicator that a client is making real progress is when they begin to visibly struggle. This process of struggling indicates you have begun to move past the part of the brain where your automatic defenses/responses live, and into the part of the brain where your emotions live—the ones that become increasingly difficult to articulate.

Step 2: Recognize Repeats

Once your Why mindset is in gear, it's time to turn back the clock. Grab another piece of paper and begin writing down the highlights/stories you can remember from both your personal and professional life—the failures, successes, heartbreaks, and achievements. This list should be long. We ask our clients to share personal stories about their family, childhood, and grade-school experiences. After years of facilitating these seminars, we find that high school is a pivotal time for leaders. Meanwhile, college is where they have learned enough about life's real-world lessons to understand the consequences of their actions. As they enter the post-college work environment, their decision-making patterns begin to solidify.

Here's a list of suggested questions to jog your memory:

1. When did you feel the greatest sense of accomplishment during your life? Career? Why?
2. Whom do you admire most? Why?
3. Who has had the greatest impact on your life? Career? Why?
4. When do you get so involved in something that you lose track of time?
5. What is the most enjoyable aspect of your life? Job? Why?
6. What do you like the least about your life? Job? Why?

When you finish answering these questions and you've written down as many highlights/stories as you can possibly think of, review your answers. Are there any age gaps or large holes, around six months or longer? If so, go back and replay your life story again. Search for more. Most of the time, the most important stories are buried deep within us. We keep them under lock and key. It is vitally important that you are vulnerable and honest with yourself in this exercise, no matter how long it takes.

Once everything has been written down, study what you have written. What are the common themes, patterns, or threads that seem to emerge? Patterns reveal an immense amount about a person. When you do this, you begin to understand what excites a leader, and it becomes increasingly easier to understand and translate the essence of their purpose back to them. When you are able to uncover the deep patterns of your life, you are able to directly align with your purpose, and that purpose becomes the magnet for strategically aligned communication, collaboration, and connection.

As you continue to study your patterns, it may be helpful to circle certain things that stand out or reoccur at different points in your life. If you see an emotion, word, skill, or activity that occurs in all of the stories, write it down on a separate sheet of paper. You may have a dozen or more themes or patterns. Then cull them down to the ones that resonate the most viscerally with you.

Do not get frustrated. This is often extremely hard to do on your own. We have had clients try many times on their own before realizing they could not get past their own subconscious defense mechanisms.

Step 3: Put Purpose to Paper

The final step is to get your *Why* down on a piece of paper to solidify it. One of the easy mistakes to make here is to confuse a How with your *Why*. So our simple framework follows a normal thinking pattern of "If I could _____, it would be great, because I could impact _____." Below is a more succinct version of this statement. Remember, your *Why* has two parts, a contribution and an impact. Your contribution is the unique way that you do what you do. Your impact is the result of the contribution you are dedicated to accomplishing. Of the many formulas one could use, we find Simon Sinek's formula the best place to start.

To _____, so that _____.
    (insert contribution)   (insert impact)

A great *Why* statement is simple and clear. A great *Why* statement lives always in service to others—clients, employees, strategic partners, and the world.

Here is Investis Digital's *Why* statement:

To create, amplify, and optimize meaningful digital communications (contribution) for the world's most ambitious brands so that they build trust and enduring relationships with their communities (impact).

Once you have drafted your *Why* statement, it's time to put it into action! Write your *Why* on a few sticky notes, then find a symbol, a color, or a photo to represent it. Practice speaking your *Why* to others. Both of these tasks most likely will feel uncomfortable at first, but they get easier with repetition. Over time, you will find yourself tweaking the language so you feel more natural as the words roll off your tongue.

To quote Don: "This part of the process right here *is* a slog. Do not get discouraged. It takes time to train your brain with new pattern language."

At this point, we are quite sure there is no need to explain what Don means when he calls this process "a slog." We also don't need to explain how invigorating and affirming finding your *Why* is. After the *Why* statement, we can turn to your values.

Identify Values

Once you have identified your purpose, you are now ready to identify the values you believe in. They serve the role of directly supporting your purpose in all aspects of your personal and professional life.

Step 1: Name Your Values

How do you identify and articulate your values? Shared values are built using both psychology and emotional intelligence. First, the process starts with identifying the strengths of the corporate visionary—you! There are countless exercises that can assist you in defining your values, but there is no shortcut here. This is one of those areas in life in which you definitely get out of it exactly what you put into it.

After constant research over the course of an entire year, reviewing the methodology of 60-plus assessments that claimed to help people identify their strengths, we discovered the CliftonStrengths assessment. (No, this isn't a paid plug, but yes, we are *huge* fans of the assessment, because it works. You can find the assessment here: www.gallup.com/cliftonstrengths.)

This assessment provides you with a wealth of information about yourself and serves as a foundational starting point for uncovering the values living within you. After taking the assessment, read the description of your top-five talent themes and highlight the phrases that viscerally resonate with you the most. CliftonStrengths is a good first step, but it is not the complete process. To really understand and embrace your values, it is important to ask those you trust a few brief questions:

- What do you come to me for?
- Why do you consider me a good friend, ally, or supporter?
- What am I best at?
- What do you trust me with the most?

Write down their answers. Receiving answers to these questions is very helpful in narrowing down your actionable core values.

Step 2: Activate the Values

Your strengths are generally adjectives or nouns, right? Someone can be resourceful or intuitive or imaginative. Someone else may possess resilience or ingenuity. But for maximum impact, your values need to be active, not just passively descriptive. For example, Fran transformed her personal strength of positivity into a shared value for her company, "Aspire Higher." Those two words are much more than just a description; they are a mindset, they are active, and they are instructive. Those two words were intentionally architected together to give every employee permission to act in alignment with this value. But the impact of Fran's shared value does not stop with employees: it specifically impacts and directs both her clients and vendors, too.

Next, create a companywide opportunity to explore personal values. First, start with your senior leadership team because this is where you will examine how (possibly) different values align and can be intentionally merged to resonate across the organization. The common core values, you share with your senior leadership team, create the shared values that define the actions of your firm going forward—all day, every day.

Step 3: Develop Accessible and Understandable Values

Once you have uncovered your firm's shared values, the next step is to create three or four sentences that spell out exactly what each value means for your company. Not doing so leaves the value open to misinterpretation. Providing employees and stakeholders those extra contextual sentences ensures that the value is institutionalized and that all stakeholders travel down the same path without veering too far off course.

Tell Your Story

The fundamental purpose of this section is to ensure you are equipped to determine if your story is purpose-oriented.

Where do you start your story? Although the story should not be self-centered, for most of our clients the initial story often begins with the leader succinctly explaining the problem the business solves. The trick to ensuring the story does not morph into a self-centered narrative is to understand the business is not the hero of the story. Instead, the hero of your story is a person with a problem. This person has similar challenges as a group of others who can easily relate. Your business is the sword that the hero uses to slay the problem.

Your story is built upon a four-part pyramid. To get there, answer these questions:

1. Who is my story's hero? What challenges does the hero face?
2. How does my business solve the hero's problem?
3. What is the direct result of my business solving the hero's problem?
4. Why is it so important to solve the hero's problem?

Here is an early draft of an Investis Digital story that does an excellent job of connecting emotionally to the reader. This story focuses on the essence of the Investis and ZOG Digital merger, without all the details:

Ben & Jerry, Fred and Ginger, Simon and Garfunkel, Jobs and Woz—the world's greatest partnerships are not always the most obvious ones. But they all have one thing in common: they combine different skills with a shared passion to create something exponentially greater. Investis is one of the world's largest and most respected corporate communications companies. With decades of experience, they have earned the trust of global leaders such as Rolls-Royce and Aflac. ZOG Digital is considered among the world's smartest and most agile digital communications firms. They are the people that hundreds of clients like KitchenAid and Wyndham turn to, in order to remain at the forefront of effective digital communications.

Investis + ZOG Digital = Investis Digital, a powerhouse corporate digital communications firm that harmonizes expertise, experience, and agility to create Connected Content—seamless digital presence across all channels that establishes meaningful, measurable connections with your audiences—customers, shareholders, employees—through consistent and effective corporate storytelling.

Every story is different. Think about how your organization is "story-living," then capture your story using the questions of the four-tiered pyramid. When you build your company story from your purpose (Why, mission, vision), and actionable values, you are simultaneously creating a historical timeline of the company's development and growth. As your understanding of your purpose and actionable values mature, the language in the company story will also mature. They are direct reflections of each other. The essence of your story will not change, but the nuances of how you tell the story may fluctuate.

We recommend revisiting all of the Three Keys at least once a year to see if any changes are required. We suggest reviewing them at annual planning events. This is usually the best time to collaborate with energized team members in a focused forum. As mentioned, you can absolutely complete these exercises on your own. However, every organization has blind spots. Better results are guaranteed when a trusted, independent expert guides a leader through the process step by step.

Acknowledgments

To say this book is by Don Scales and Fran Biderman Gross overstates the case. Significant contributions have been made by some incredibly important and amazing people, and without their support this book would certainly not exist.

To the man who made the impossible possible, Clay Hebert, thank you.

Your support and perspectives were invaluable: David Linn, Zachary Herskowitz, Kristen Kalupski, and Gary Whitehill.

An amazing team keeps us on our toes and in our lane: Barbara Boyd, Janet Murnaghan, Kacy Wren, Michael Gormley, Jeanenne Ray, and Vicki Adang.

Fran's Acknowledgments

Thank you for always filling me with inspiring words and thoughts, Warren Rustand and Seth Goden. To the man who has only one volume, you are my swim coach, Jack Daly. Simon Sinek, what impact your "little idea" has had.

To our incredible team at Advantages, past and present, who have and will continue to Aspire Higher: Angelica "Jelly," Cesar, Luly, Ruthie, Jaclyn, Courtney, Sam, Ana, Gabriella, Stephanie, Danielle, Tony, Joe, Neil, Derek, Kevin, Jerry, Rachel, Kayla, Rosa, Bracha, and Christel.

To Yeeshai Jesse Marcus Gross, the man whose purpose in life is to create impactful and memorable moments, constantly raising the bar, always pushing—I mean encouraging—me to do even more. I am grateful and blessed to have found love twice. You are my rock. Yes, you make me laugh.

To my incredible children—whom I live for and am most proud of, still my biggest accomplishment to date—maybe writing this book was harder than giving birth because I will remember it: Avinoam Biderman, D'vora Biderman, and Ariella Gross.

Nicole Biderman—you truly are a bonus! Yes, all sales are final.

To the woman who gives me the most reason never to worry, thank you, Glenesha Israel. Our family has nothing but an abundance of love for you.

Dad, Bernie Leff, you always told me that I was the best investment. You are the ultimate Poppy.

Mom, you display the ultimate in kindness every day. Thank you for that constant lesson.

To my "bad ass" sister, Deborah Freund, and sparkly brother-in-law, Chaim, may we never stop learning from one another, supporting one another, and may we always continue to grow closer.

Sevek, who always knows a way, and never ceases to amaze me with the amount of expert knowledge you retain.

Kim Harrison, who truly understands how to help others revel in who they really are.

Susan Lindner, you hold up a mirror better than anyone I know. I love you for it. I will always be your best Fran.

Maika Leibbrandt, we are kindred sisters who only know how to play to our strengths to disrupt all we know.

Zvi Gluck, may you always have the strength to do what you do. You truly accomplish the impossible.

Tom Grech, you are a leader among men paving the way for greatness in our amazing city.

Grandma Ruth, you know the everlasting impression you have made on me, your first grandchild. You are deeply missed, and continue to inspire me each and every day. Yes Grandma, I am pointing my finger right at you, and wishing most of all that you were here in person and I know how proud you would be to see this.

Don's Acknowledgments

To Fran Crumpton, my tenth-grade English teacher and my mom's best friend, a part of my family and my life coach as far back as I can remember.

To all the loyal people with whom I have had the honor and privilege to work every day for the past thirty-plus years. You know who you are. This book would not be possible if it weren't for your support.

But most importantly, to my closest personal friends, who give me daily encouragement in life. Your love and unconditional support are what keeps me moving forward every day. Thank you for everything.

Index